Social Justice for the Oppressed

Social Justice for the Oppressed

Critical Educators and Intellectuals Speak Out

Pierre Wilbert Orelus

ROWMAN & LITTLEFIELD
Lanham • Boulder • New York • London

Published by Rowman & Littlefield
A wholly owned subsidiary of The Rowman & Littlefield Publishing Group, Inc.
4501 Forbes Boulevard, Suite 200, Lanham, Maryland 20706
www.rowman.com

Unit A, Whitacre Mews, 26-34 Stannary Street, London SE11 4AB

British Library Cataloguing in Publication Information Available

Library of Congress Cataloging-in-Publication Data

Names: Orelus, Pierre W., author.
Title: Social justice for the oppressed : critical educators and intellectuals speak out / Pierre Wilbert
    Orelus.
Description: Lanham, Maryland : Rowman & Littlefield, 2017.
Identifiers: LCCN 2016052622 (print) | LCCN 2017002337 (ebook) | ISBN 9781475804478 (cloth :
    alk. paper) | ISBN 9781475804485 (pbk : alk. paper) | ISBN 9781475804492 (electronic)
Subjects: LCSH: Social justice. | Minorities. | Discrimination.
Classification: LCC HM671 .O73 2017 (print) | LCC HM671 (ebook) | DDC 303.3/72—dc23
LC record available at https://lccn.loc.gov/2016052622

∞ ™ The paper used in this publication meets the minimum requirements of American
National Standard for Information Sciences Permanence of Paper for Printed Library
Materials, ANSI/NISO Z39.48-1992.

Printed in the United States of America

Contents

Foreword

Love, Joy, and Justice

William Ayers

Like every muscular, compelling, and layered concept, *social justice* is difficult to sum up and quite impossible to define definitively. More process than calculation, more journey than destination, social justice is an impulse that resists easy answers and defies breezy responses. There is simply no getting to the bottom of it, once and for all—social justice is too dynamic, too dense, too on-the-move and in-the-mix. It demands careful and sustained examination, and that's precisely why *Social Justice for the Oppressed* is irreplaceable.

Here eleven engaged activist thinkers—from Kevin Kumashiro and Maxine Greene to Stuart Hall and Noam Chomsky—participate in conversation with Pierre Wilbert Orelus, exploring the idea of social justice from a wide range of perspectives, standpoints, and experiences. As they dive into the conflicts and contradictions of their own work, each interlocutor vitalizes the idea of social justice for the rest of us and simultaneously illuminates the central struggles of our time. Perhaps just as important, they illustrate the unmistakable power of dialogue: opening our eyes and our ears with the possibility of being changed, and speaking up and acting out with the possibility of being heard. This is propulsive and essential reading for teachers and scholars, organizers and activists. You will find insights, revelations, and provocations on every page.

Social justice can be thrilling and just as often surprising and disorienting because it stretches toward the infinite, embracing the far-flung strivings of wildly diverse peoples in different times and places, under vastly different circumstances, using different tools and tactics and methods and approaches to achieve greater freedom, fairness, equity, access, agency, openness, sustainability, and recognition. That human striving, that hunger for justice, is awakened when people recognize, often fleetingly or glancingly at first, that the forces pressing down upon us—forces of oppression and exploitation, racism and discrimination, displacement and erasure, pestilence and plague—are neither natural nor immutable. We open our eyes and notice that things could be otherwise; we resist; we rise up angry.

Awareness and wide-awakeness—this is the starting point of struggles for justice, but it is not the end. We allow ourselves a sense of wonder and astonishment: there is loveliness all around us, aching beauty, yes, and flashes of ecstasy; there is horror in every direction as well, appalling injustices and pain, the unnecessary suffering we humans visit upon one another. We feel the need to speak up and act out, and the rhythm of rebellion: pay attention; be astonished; act. Add the need to doubt that whatever you saw or did or said was adequate or complete, and then the charge to rethink and start over, and you've got the rhythm of revolution: pay attention, be astonished, act up, and doubt. Repeat for a lifetime.

To be enslaved is to be measured and assessed, inspected and counted, evaluated and regulated, admonished and corrected, indoctrinated and reformed, threatened and prodded and punished. It's to have your agency ignored or constrained or systematically crushed. To trudge toward freedom is to overthrow all of that through self-activity, an insurgency that involves seizing and practicing your own agency, stepping into history not as an object—a fraction of a human, or three-fifths of a person—not as a label or a collection of deficits or someone else's imposed statistical profile, but as a fully realized and three-dimensional human being.

The social justice activists in conversation in these pages have been moved again and again to defend the weak, to defy oppressive or even imperfect authority, to criticize orthodoxy and dogma, stereotype and received wisdom of every kind. They are freedom fighters who lean against the idea that life or learning must be an arid, dry, self-referencing and self-satisfied affair, a mechanical trivial pursuit of the obvious; they resist deference, didacticism, ego, and complacency in a heartless world, prisons and border guards and walls—whether in our own minds or in the lives of our students, whether in Texas or in Palestine—and quarantines, deletions, and closures. They welcome the unknown, the marvelous, the poetics of resistance, history, and agency. They provide frames for mapping a world that could be but is not yet, a place of joy and justice, powered by love.

—**William Ayers**, Distinguished Professor of Education, Senior University Scholar, University of Illinois at Chicago (retired)

Acknowledgments

This volume would not have been materialized without the genuine contribution of all educators and intellectuals involved in it. I wish to thank them all for their time, knowledge, and expertise. I will always be grateful to them. Second, my deep gratitude goes to the staff at Rowman & Littlefield, particularly Sarah Jubar, who was very patient and understanding as I was working on the manuscript. Third, thank you to all oppressed groups who have inspired me to write this book. Finally, I am thankful to my wife, Romina Pacheco, and my daughter, Asha Orelus-Pacheco, who have been extremely supportive and patient throughout the long process of finishing this book over six years. You two are my rock and always will be!

Introduction

The range of social justice issues (often called "isms" for short) illustrates the view held by social justice educators that there are many sources of inequality and injustice, that these manifestations of oppression often interact with each other, that inequality or injustice cannot be eliminated by focus on one form of oppression solely, and that there is no hierarchy of importance among these forms of oppression.

Although one or another manifestation of oppression may be more visible in a specific context, all are salient to those groups that experience advantage as well as disadvantage on the basis of a specific "ism." (Adams, as cited in Chapman & Hobbel, 2010, p. 63). Social justice in the curriculum must be rooted in a sense of hope, connected to the future, solidarity with others, and a willingness to fight for what one believes in.

Last but not least, social justice can frame our work as educators only to the degree that it connects with the experiences and histories of the students we teach and work with (Giroux, as cited in Ayers et al., 1998, p. 291). Teaching for social justice, we must remember, is teaching what we believe ought to be—not merely moral frameworks are concerned, but material arrangements for people in all spheres of society.

Moreover, teaching for social justice is teaching for the sake of arousing the kinds of vivid, reflective, experiential responses that might move students to come together in serious efforts to understand what social justice actually means and what it might demand (Greene, as cited in Ayers et al., 1998, p. 291).

These days, social justice is evoked in various contexts and circles, and often influences controversial debates centered on social, economic, political, educational, and environmental issues. Both convergent and mismatched interests frequently inform these debates. Despite the common use of social justice in public debates shaping the mainstream media narrative, for example, it is often misunderstood or interpreted variably by people.

It can mean something at times drastically different to individuals and groups depending on their vested personal, socioeconomic, ideological, political, and educational interests. People's view of, and stance on, social justice is often influenced by their varying degree of lived experiences, beliefs, and set of family values. People's religious faith, gender, social class, race, and sex privileges (or not) also influence their views of, and stance on, social justice issues.

For instance, the way heterosexual, Christian, conservative, and able-bodied upper middle class people understand social justice might differ from the way historically oppressed groups understand or define it. For these groups, social justice, as praxis, does not reflect in the oppressive manner in which they have been historically treated in society. In other words, what social justice means to highly privileged groups or individuals in society is different for those who have been historically oppressed.

In fact, to the latter, social justice is yet to mean something meaningful and substantive. Many people have been victims of social injustice. Victims of social injustice include those bullied by their partners, relatives, professors, teachers, peers, colleagues, and coworkers. It is no exaggeration to state that we commit social injustices against one another, whether we are conscious of it or not, or whether we want to admit it or not. We commit injustices against one another because of our fear, insecurity, envy, jealousy, greed, arrogance, ignorance, and bigotry of some kind.

Many individuals lecture on social justice, equity, and fairness, yet disappoint others by their inappropriate or even hostile behavior, biased judgment, and unfair treatment of other people. Discussions on social justice must entail the examination of unequal power relations between groups and individuals as well as mistreatment of others stemming from systemic forms of oppression, which cause deep sufferings to oppressed groups, including students, lingering at times for decades.

While we yet have to live in a just society, where people are not discriminated against because of their race, sexual orientation, social class, and religious beliefs, mainstream discourse on social justice continues to be spread through the corporate media, schools, churches, and the public sphere. This discourse works for the powerful. As for oppressed groups, they have yet to see social justice mean something substantive to their daily lives.

To put it simply, a propagandistic, mainstream, and neoliberal notion of social justice does not serve the interest of the wretched of the earth (Fanon, 1963). Therefore, more honest, courageous, and committed educators and public intellectuals need to be involved in dialogues exploring these issues, which this book offers. And most importantly, more sociopolitical movements, like the Black Lives Matter, Immigrant Rights, and LGBTQ movements in the United States, fighting for social justice need to emerge. There is an urgent need for the emergence or increase of *social justice praxiers*.

By *social justice praxiers*, I mean individuals who not only eloquently talk about social justice issues but also make a genuine effort to apply them to their daily lives, including the humane and respectful way they interact with and treat others and are involved in some forms of activism in their community conducive to social change. To put it simply, *social justice praxiers* are individuals or groups who critically reflect on and then transform theoretical knowledge about social justice into praxis serving humanity.

WHY SOCIAL JUSTICE FOR THE OPPRESSED NOW?

Social justice is a popular term, and as such surfaces in discussions revolved around equity, fairness, and equality issues, including equal distribution of and access to resources among people. The most common questions emerging from such discussions include: (1) Whose interests does social justice serve? (2) How does it look in segregated schools, targeted and disfranchised communities? What is the color of social justice in occupied lands?

What does it mean to historically oppressed groups and people, such as Native Americans, African Americans, Blacks, Latinos/as, Palestinians, Muslims, Jews, and other oppressed groups? And what is it like for queer individuals and women? As will be further illustrated later in this introduction and the book as a whole, one's gender, socioeconomic, sexual orientation, racial, and linguistic backgrounds, as well as ideological and political positions inform one's understanding of, and stance on, social justice issues. Nieto (2010) notes,

> Social justice: it's on everyone's minds these days. From political pundits to teacher educators, from school principals to parents, and from political scientists to car salespeople, everyone has an opinion on social justice. Some are staunch advocates, others fierce opponents, but everyone seems passionate about the promise or the perils of social justice. Some consider it the sine qua non of a democracy. Others liken it to socialism and the end of civilized world as we know it. But what is social justice? (cited in Chapman & Hobbel, p. iv)

Discussions revolved around social justice issues should compel one to ask broader pertinent questions, such as: Who gets to attend well-resourced schools and has access to quality education, and why? Who attends underfunded schools, and why? Who has access to decent-paying jobs with good benefits and who does not, and why? Who gets promoted at work, and on what criteria do people in superior positions base promotions for those from subaltern positions? Who has access to quality health care—if any—and who does not, and why?

Who most likely will get killed by police officers on the street, receive an unfair trial, go to jail, or receive the death penalty, and why? Whose languages and cultures are valued or looked down upon in schools, and why? Whose tongue has been tied in schools, particularly in classroom settings, and why? Who gets to speak, and on behalf of whom? In churches, who are in key positions, and what kind of conversations are occurring therein? Who often joins the army, who holds prestigious ranks therein, who receives better treatment and gets promoted, and why?

In short, whom has social justice benefited? And whom has it not served? These are fundamental questions that merit deep and critical examination. Besides schools, churches, and the army, social injustice takes place in our legal system. Poor black and brown people, particularly African American and Latino males, make up the majority of inmates in the U.S. prison system (Alexander, 2010).

According to Alexander, the majority of these inmates—often caged in prisons for minor offenses—are subjected to a second-class citizen status, experiencing employment discrimination and other forms of discrimination upon their release from jails (Alexander, 2010). While grand rhetoric about social justice and human rights from political pundits is floating in the mainstream media and at the United Nations, people in occupied and neocolonized lands, like Palestine, Afghanistan, Iraq, Tibet, and Haiti, respectively, continue to be experiencing the effects of Western imperialism, occupation, neocolonization, and violence of war because of Western countries' socioeconomic and geopolitical interests.

Similarly, despite some gains and successes by the women's and LGBTQ's movements—women like Hillary Clinton and Condoleezza Rice have been able to occupy key political positions, while some gay and lesbian couples have been allowed to marry in some states in the United States—women and queer people continue to be among the most marginalized groups in society. Finally, thanks to the civil rights movement, African Americans and other Blacks are now legally allowed to vote in the United States. However, there has been a mechanism put in place in some U.S. states, like Florida, to prevent them from freely exercising this right as citizens of a nation that takes pride in calling itself the land of the free or a democratic land. Various forms of social injustices that have been committed against historically oppressed groups show clearly the failed U.S. democracy and biased legal system.

Social injustice leads to human suffering, misery, and various forms of violence—emblematic, psychological, emotional, physical, sexual, spiritual, and economic, to which oppressed groups have been subjected. People subjected to various forms of social injustices often suffer long-term psychological effects. While lofty speeches on freedom, social justice, and democracy are promoted in the mainstream, oppression continues to occur, affecting the livelihood of historically oppressed people.

Unless systemic forms of oppression are uprooted, social injustice of some kind will continue to affect them. Social justice for the oppressed can't be delayed, given their precarious conditions. It needs to happen now, as it is already deferred. This book provides a critical examination of social injustice issues, including the manner in which race-, class-, language-, and gender-based discrimination intersect to affect oppressed groups. This book goes on to propose alternative ways to counter social injustice in schools and society at large.

Eleven prominent social justice educators and public intellectuals were interviewed for this purpose. These educators and intellectuals provide important insights and alternative progressive views on many social justice issues aforementioned. This book uses interviews as an alternative genre to unveil systemic forms of oppression occurring in schools and society at large. By *unveil* is meant taking off deep and thick ideological layers and dominant discourses aimed to cover social injustices perpetrated by those in power.

Interviews have historically been used as an oral analytical tool to denounce injustices while at the same time inspiring deep creative and philosophical thoughts in the mind and consciousness of the reader or the listener. This book uses interviews to expose injustices, aiming to provoke human outrage leading to the creation and emergence of social movements fighting for structural economic, educational, social, and political change.

The scholarly and activist works of intellectuals interviewed for this book have critically analyzed and denounced social injustices. I call these intellectuals the borderless talented tenth of the twenty-first century, for they cross racial, cultural, linguistic, and ideological borders to analyze and expose social justice issues to readers and listeners beyond their disciplines and the wall of the ivory tower.

THE BORDERLESS TALENTED TENTH: AN OVERVIEW

The term *talented tenth* goes back to the nineteenth century. Specifically, this term was coined by a group of white liberals in the Northern part of the United States who wanted to build colleges aimed at training black teachers to educate and inspire black schoolchildren and other blacks. A century later or so, the prominent African American intellectual W. E. B. DuBois appropriated this term, arguing that one in ten black men should occupy leadership positions in the black communities and be involved in intellectual and sociopolitical movements leading to social change (Du-Bois, 1903).

Unlike his contemporary, Booker T. Washington, who believed that blacks should receive an industrial type of education and training to advance economically and become independent (Washington, 1903), Du-Bois believed that receiving a classical education would help blacks elevate themselves intellectually and professionally, so that they were prepared to compete with Whites. DuBois's *talented tenth* term has been contested. In *Transcending the Talented Tenth*, James (1997) challenges this term.

He argues that the term is too elitist and limiting and therefore fails to acknowledge multiple talented leaders and intellectuals of different rankings existing in the black community. Toward the end of his life, DuBois

(1986) realized that leadership does not emerge only from elite groups but also from people involved in grassroots organizations and movements. He stated, "My own panacea of earlier days was flight of class from mass through the development of the Talented Tenth, but the power of this aristocracy of talent was to lie in its knowledge and character, not its wealth" (p. 842).

My use of the term *talented tenth* in this introduction is contextually and ideologically different from that of DuBois. By calling intellectuals involved in this book "the borderless talented tenth," I am specifically alluding to the fact that they are world-leading intellectual authorities from various gender, racial, ethnic, linguistic, social class, and sexual backgrounds who have transcended their respective disciplines to explore in their academic, scholarly, and activist work social issues concerning humankind.

Indeed, these intellectuals have transgressed racial, cultural, and gender boundaries to engage issues affecting humanity. They have had a deep influence on people across continents from diverse cultural, racial, social class, linguistic, and academic backgrounds; they have embraced causes aimed at serving humanity as a whole.

THE INTERVIEWED INTELLECTUALS AND EDUCATORS

Every one hundred years or more we have witnessed the emergence of a few giant intellectuals across continents, whose scholarly and activist work has transcended academic confines and challenged the boundaries of pedagogical and political discourses. The scholars invited to take part in this book are undeniably the most prominent among these intellectuals.

The substantial amount of scholarly work they have produced over several decades combined with their activism have profoundly influenced scholars of their generations and present generations, and will undoubtedly inspire future generations of scholars and activists. Invited scholars to this book are transcending intellectuals reaching audiences far beyond their respective disciplines.

Their well-substantiated views on social justice issues facing people, particularly the poor and the oppressed, might enable the reader to develop a deeper understanding of broader socioeconomic and political underlying factors leading, for example, to wealth disparity and linguistic and racial apartheid among uneven groups. Some of the interviewees are members of disfranchised groups that have personally witnessed and experienced egregious violation of people's human rights throughout their personal and professional journey.

Many of them know firsthand how it feels to be discriminated against because of their class, gender, race, nationality, and sex. The social justice educators interviewed for this book have written for decades about social justice from varying theoretical, epistemological, pedagogical, and political standpoints. While some have examined this concept from a postcolonial and Marxist perspective, others have looked at it through a feminist, educational, and humanistic lens.

However, they all agree on the following basic premise: all individuals, including students, deserve an equal chance and adequate support to fulfill their potentials and succeed academically and in life in general. This basic premise can be translated into reality for everyone if we collectively fight to eradicate social inequality and prejudices of all kinds, which should be part of our social justice political projects.

CONTEXTUALIZING THE BOOK

This anthology is inspired by a previous anthology, *Rethinking Race, Class, Language, and Gender: A Dialogue with Noam Chomsky and Other Leading Scholars*, which I authored about five years ago (Orelus, 2011). Like the first anthology, this one examines the ways and the degree to which race, language, class, and gender intersect to influence life opportunities, distribution of resources among diverse groups, student learning outcomes, and socioeconomic, racial, linguistic, and sexual conditions of people.

This book captures the voices and novel views of public and world-renowned intellectuals and social justice educators across generations, who are from different racial, gender, academic, and professional backgrounds; sexual orientations; and religious backgrounds. These scholars and educators are steadfastly committed to social justice issues, as reflected in their scholarly work, teaching, and sociopolitical activism.

BOOK ORGANIZATION

This book has two major sections examining interwoven issues. Because the scholars involved in this book are borderless intellectuals writing and speaking about intersecting forms of oppression, the content of both sections overlaps. That is, similar issues are addressed in both sections, albeit from different theoretical, ideological, and epistemological standpoints. A cautiously crafted epigrammatic introduction precedes each section to provide the reader a general idea of interviews included within. This introduction places all of the interviews in broader sociopolitical and educational context.

CONCLUSION

Given its focus, this book holds relevance to educators, students, professionals, and citizens in general who are concerned with social justice issues, including social justice education. This book might also be of interest to those interested in multicultural education and critical race theory. Finally, this book might be of interest to students majoring in sociology and political science.

REFERENCES

Adams, M. (2010). "Roots of Social Justice Pedagogies in Social Movements." In T. Chapman & N. Hobbel (Eds.), *Social Justice Pedagogy across the Curriculum: The Practice of Freedom* (pp. 36–85). New York: Routledge.

Bell, D. (1980). "Brown v. Board of Education and the Interest-Convergence Dilemma." *Harvard Law Review* 93(3), 518–33.

Collins, P. H. (2000). *Black Feminist Thought: Knowledge, Consciousness, and the Politics of Empowerment* (2nd ed.). New York: Routledge.

DuBois, W. E. B. (1986). "Writings." In *Dusk of Dawn* (p. 842). Library of America.

DuBois, W. E. B. (1903). "The Talented Tenth," September 1903, TeachingAmericanHistory.org, Ashland University, accessed September 3, 2008.

Early, G., & Kennedy, R. (Eds.) (2010). *Best African American Essays*. New York: One World Books.

Giroux, H. (1998). "An Activist Forum V: Racing Social Justice." In J. Ayers, J. A. Hunt, and T. Quinn, (Eds.), *Teaching for Social Justice* (pp. 290–91). New York: Teachers College Press.

Greene, M. (1998). Introduction. In J. Ayers, J. A. Hunt, and T. Quinn (Eds.), *Teaching for Social Justice* (pp. xxvii–xlvi). New York: Teachers College Press.

Hardiman, R., Jackson, B., & Griffin, P. (2007). "Conceptual Foundations for Social Justice Education." In M. Adams, L. A. Bell, & P. Griffin (Eds.), *Teaching for Diversity and Social Justice* (2nd ed.) (pp. 35–66). New York: Routledge.

hooks, b. (1981). *Ain't I a Woman*. Cambridge, MA: South End Press.

hooks, b. (1989). *Talking Back: Thinking Feminist, Thinking Black*. Boston, MA: South End Press.

James, J. (1997). *Transcending the Talented Tenth: Black Leaders and American Intellectuals*. New York: Routledge.

Kohl, H. (1998). "Some Reflections of Teaching for Social Justice (Afterword)." In J. Ayers, J. A. Hunt, & T. Quinn (Eds.), *Teaching for Social Justice* (pp. 285–87). New York: Teachers College Press.

Kumashiro, K. (2009). Foreword. In E. N. Conne (Ed.), *Teaching for Social Justice: Voices from the Front Lines*. Boulder, CO: Paradigm Publishers.

Nieto, S. (2010). Foreword. In T. Chapman & N. Hobbel (Eds.), *Social Justice Pedagogy across the Curriculum: The Practice of Freedom*. New York: Routledge.

Orelus, P. W. (Ed.) (Summer 2011). *Rethinking Race, Class, Language, and Gender: A Dialogue with Noam Chomsky and Other Leading Scholars*. Lanham, MD: Rowman & Littlefield.

Shierholz, H., & Could, E. (2011). "Poverty and Income Trends Continue to Paint a Bleak Picture for Working Families." Retrieved from Economic Policy Institute, http://www.epi.org/publication/lost-decade-poverty-income-trends-continue.

Tatum, B. D. (2007). *Can We Talk about Race? And Other Conversations in an Era of School Resegregation*. Boston, MA: Beacon Press.

Washington, B. T. (1903). *The Negro Problem: A Series of Articles by Representative American Negroes of Today*. New York: James Pott and Company.

I

Overview

Social justice encompasses all issues concerning humanity. While some are race, class, gender, and language related, others include sexuality, homophobia, xenophobia, and religion, to name just a few. Social justice is pervasive, and shapes public and political discourses and debates centered on such topics as globalization, war, AIDS, sex trafficking, and child and elderly abuses. Other public debates revolving around social justice issues include marriage equality and equal rights for minorities.

Equal and fair pay for women and bridging the resource gap between affluent and nondominant students are also embedded in the educational and political debates focusing on social justice issues. In addition, opportunity disparities leading to unequal power relations between dominant and oppressed groups have been part of social justice debates. Finally, Western occupation of other countries and the effects of such occupation on the occupied has been given center stage in social justice debates.

This section showcases prominent public intellectuals, scholars, and educators, such as Noam Chomsky, Rodolfo Acuna, Gayatri Chakravorty Spivak, and Antonia Darder, who have written extensively about the way marginalized groups have been ravaged by Western imperialism, classism, sexism, and racism. They also tackle issues including opportunity gaps affecting the living conditions of oppressed groups, including students. Moreover, they denounce the exploitation of the poor by corporations; in short, they unmask race, class, language, and gender oppression, among others.

In their analysis, they not only point out ways in which socioeconomic, racial, social class, and linguistic factors might have affected the lives of historically oppressed groups, but they also provide examples demonstrating the manner and extent to which these groups have used their agency and spirit of resilience to fight against their oppressor. The issues these scholars critically analyze in this section often get superficially talked about in the mainstream media but not as in-depth as they are here in this book.

Their stance on social justice issues is timely, as it challenges orthodox types of beliefs about these issues while at the same time denouncing discriminatory practices many oppressed groups have been subjected to. The wide range of scholarship, political activism, encyclopedic knowledge, and existential experiences of these intellectuals and educators place them in a unique position to engage these social justice issues and shed light on them.

They speak quite candidly and knowledgeably about both the hope and perils of social justice at a time when targeted groups, like African Americans, Arabs, especially those who are Muslims, and immigrants of color have been under attack by extremist xenophobic and racist groups, like the KKK in the United States, supporting the far-ultra-right-wing American president, Donald Trump, who has been an inspirational voice for them.

While President Trump and other political pundits alike have already been making lofty promises to the general public to gain their consent in order to secure their votes in the next presidential election, many students continue to attend underfunded schools located in unsafe and poor neighborhoods and millions are unemployed and/or incarcerated. This book intends to serve as an entry dialogical point to address these social justice issues.

ONE

Re-envisioning Social Justice and Democracy

Noam Chomsky Speaks

Orelus: Let me begin by saying that the main focus of this dialogue is social justice. With that said, let me ask you the following question: In what way do you feel that social justice, as broadly defined, has informed your work?

Chomsky: It's the main thing I work on. Virtually everything I do in the activist social political realm is falling under the concept of social justice.

Orelus: Can you tell me more about that?

Chomsky: Opposition to aggression, difference to protect human rights. Just about everything. I just came back from Gaza a couple of days ago; that's motivated by the first visit there; and the work I do is motivated by concern for the rights of the people; that's social justice. I stopped in Egypt on the way to Gaza and gave talks on situations in the Arab world; and that's again motivated by the idea that people should be able to have their legitimate rights. I can't think of anything that wouldn't fall under social justice.

Orelus: You have written and spoken extensively about a wide range of issues such as Western imperialism, particularly U.S. imperialism. You have also talked about democracy and globalization. These are issues people should be concerned about. To what extent do you think these issues are connected to social justice?

3

Chomsky: They're all connected. For example, let's take democracy. A country is democratic to the extent that its population plays a role in determining policy. This is a good measure of democracy. And the role of the public, if it had a role, would be to promote their rights and justice and organize to have an accurate perception of the world. So the two are closely related. Imperialism is obviously domination and control to undermine social justice.

As far as globalization is concerned, we have to be careful about what we're talking about. There are several versions of globalization. There is the kind of globalization symbolized by the simultaneous meetings for the last ten years at Davos, Switzerland. People attending the World Social Forum in Brazil and India, where we happened to be meeting, are committed to globalization, but a different kind. The Davos meetings are the people who are sometimes called the Masters of the Universe. They are the investor class, the banks, the powerful states that cater to their interests and so on. This is a particular version of globalization, which is designed primarily to promote investor rights, corporate rights, power of the wealthy, and so on. That's what's called globalization because they are the dominant force.

The World Social Forum is also concerned with globalization. It's sometimes called alternative globalization; they're concerned with the rights of people. And if you attend the World Social Forum meeting, you'll realize that it's drawn from people all over the world with different social classes and vocations; they are farmers, workers, women, and others. They are concerned with trying to create a world system which will respond to the needs of people. That's another kind of globalization. Well, for the powerful and the elite, that's not called globalization because they don't run the international information system.

Orelus: Noam, in your talks focusing on U.S. foreign policy, you have eloquently and critically talked about how certain countries, particularly developing countries, have been affected both economically and politically by U.S. foreign policy. So in your opinion, what are some of the long-term socioeconomic, educational, and political effects of this policy on the lives of marginalized groups living in developing countries?

Chomsky: Well, the United States essentially picked up where the European imperialism left off. Up to the Second World War the United States was the richest country in the world. It wasn't a major actor in world affairs. It was nearby, like in the Western hemisphere, but not globally. Britain was the major actor after the Second World War that changed for obvious reasons. The United States took over the effort to control the world in the interest of Western power. Britain became a junior partner, as they called themselves, and of course the consequences for the world are generally negative, not surprisingly.

Powerful states act in the interest of their own internal sources of domestic power. And the effect on others is incidental sometimes; sometimes it may harm. But it certainly isn't designed to improve their interests. In fact, the whole First World and Third World divide traces back to early Western imperialism. In the eighteenth century the gap between what's now called the First and the Third World was not very great. By now it is, of course; it's huge. And that's a result of who has the guns.

Orelus: So what would you propose be done, Noam, to counter the negative effects of U.S. imperialism on these countries?

Chomsky: Two things. First of all, they have to take their own fate into their own hands and move toward independence and some serious internal development. For example, Latin America has done that to an important extent in the last ten years. That's a historically significant achievement. That's after five hundred years of subordination to Western power. So partly it's internal and partly it has to be internal to the United States. The World Social Forum is a place where concerned citizens meet and work together. Together they offer more opportunities and freedom to people in the world to pursue their own concerns without foreign domination.

Orelus: Speaking of domination, as I was going through many of your books that I have bought and have been reading for the last ten years, I came across one that caught my attention: Hegemony or Survival. *So I'm curious to know what exactly do you mean by that? What prompted your decision to attribute this title to this book? What exactly do you mean by hegemony or survival?*

Chomsky: Hegemony is just the standard word for global domination in the interest of domestic power systems. That's one option we can pursue. There are serious questions of survival, including survival of the species. As discussed in that book, there are two major threats to survival and a lot of minor ones. The major threats are environmental catastrophe and nuclear war. And they remain very serious threats. As long as U.S. policy is directed toward hegemony, it's going to threaten survival. So we have a choice. Which one is it going to be?

Orelus: Well, it all depends on where one stands and whose interests are in danger. I'm going to shift from U.S. foreign policy to language issues. As you know, many bilingual and multilingual students continue to be punished in

*school for speaking their native tongues, especially with the abolishment of
the bilingual program in the state where you're currently living, Massachusetts, as well as in Arizona, California, and so on. How do you explain this
form of linguistic intolerance or, if I may, this form of linguistic apartheid?
And what does that really say to you as a linguist in terms of the political
nature of the U.S. school system?*

Chomsky: Well, that's really not a linguistic question; it's a social justice question. People should have the right to speak their own language; to have their own culture; to help it become a flourishing culture, a lively language, and so on. And I think that's healthy for the
society as a whole. However, there are very strong native entitlements
that persist and take many forms, including racism.

Anti-immigrant supporters have always tried to preserve their image
of what's called a white Anglo-Saxon society. This runs right through
American history for obvious reasons. Those supporting a white Anglo-Saxon society participated in the elimination of the Indigenous
population. The influx of immigrants pouring into the rich country
from abroad has threatened those in power. They are going to be a
minority of the population pretty soon. And this is causing a lot of
hatred, fear, and anger.

I'm sure a lot of the hysteria about Obama comes from that. It's not
just the people dislike him. They're hysterical about it. The popular
views about Obama's place of birth are unbelievable. I may have the
figures wrong, but my recollection is that in the latest polls, 40 percent
of Americans think that Obama was born in the United States. This is
outlandish. A very small percentage, maybe a third or so percent of
the population believe he's a Christian. About half of Republicans
think that he intends to impose Islamic law not just on the United
States but on the whole world. I mean that's actual lunacy.

Actually, a quarter of Republicans think that he might be anti-Christ.
These are views that you just can't find anywhere else in the world.
But it's a large part of the U.S. culture. And it goes way back and in
many ways is becoming more frightening as the society becomes more
diverse and complex. The power and role of the traditional ruling
sector is diminishing.

*Orelus: The gap between the so-called Standard English and languages such
as Spanish, Haitian Creole, and Vietnamese is getting wider every day. So
what would you propose be done to bridge this gap?*

Chomsky: Usual story, political activism in some places. For example, I
was in Arizona a while ago. Arizona, which basically I refer to as

occupied Mexico. Texas, Arizona, Southwest, and generally the West Coast were just conquered territories, and there are plenty of Mexicans. That's why you have Spanish place names. San Diego, San Francisco, Santa Cruz, and so on are occupied Mexico. Plenty of Mexicans are living there. Now there are Mexican Americans.

While I was there, the Arizona legislature had just forced the closing of a very successful Chicana/o studies program. They had actually gone as far as banning books like *The Tempest*, because it has anticolonial character to it; they banned Chicano history, historical work on Columbus. That's really pretty extreme but that's Arizona. Places like Massachusetts are doing other things like opposing bilingual education.

Orelus: You are considered one of the world's leading linguists. In your opinion, Noam, to what degree have language studies contributed to improve the cultural, linguistic, and material conditions of the less fortunate or, if I may borrow Frantz Fanon's phrase, the wretched of the earth?

Chomsky: Well, it's different answers in different places. Take Haiti, for example, where the language of the people is Creole but the language of the elite is French. You know better than I do about this. Creole has been undermined in many ways through publications, official usage, and textbooks, all kinds of things. In fact, it is denounced as not really a language, which is ridiculous. It's as much of a language as French. Of course that's very harmful to the cultural and the socioeconomic life of the Haitian people.

Take Turkey as another example. Right now there's been harsh oppression of Kurds for years, but it's picking up again. Kurds are a very large minority in Turkey, and they want the right to speak their own language, to have their own radio programs, their own schools, and to some degree their autonomy. This has been destroyed by a fear of massive violence. It was improving for a while, but now it's getting worse—dozens of journalists and others are in jail. All of this is undermining the linguistic, cultural, and political rights of a very large segment of the population. These things are happening everywhere.

Spain is another example. The debate over the use of Catalan is happening. Under the Franco dictatorship Catalan was banned. You couldn't have a street sign in Catalan. After Franco was finally kicked out and died, Catalan surfaced again. Of course people have already spoken it not just officially but also publicly. It's now the language of the region and it's moved on to the pressures of its revival; cultural practices like dancing and singing are done in Catalan.

Orelus: Given your descriptive and critical analysis of the language situation in Haiti, Turkey, and Spain, what would you propose be done in order to live in a society that is linguistically and socially just?

Chomsky: Too many things to enumerate. I mean we could make a long list of rights that ought to be recognized and secured for the entire population. In fact the Universal Declaration of Human Rights is a good start. That includes cultural rights. That's one third of it. It also includes socioeconomic rights and political rights. It's not perfect, but it's quite a good start.

Orelus: You have referred to the Universal Declaration of Human Rights as a starting point. But from your own standpoint as a linguist and political activist, what would you propose be done to counteract these social wrongs?

Chomsky: I don't think there's a single answer for every situation. It depends on circumstances. In Haiti, Creole should be the national language. In Turkey, Kurdish should be an accepted, supported language, which people should be permitted to freely use. In the United States, the Spanish-speaking community should have a right to bilingual education in pursuit of Hispanic culture, if they want to. And there are different answers in different places.

Orelus: What role should public intellectuals play in building a society where one language is respected and valued? What should we do as teachers, public intellectuals?

Chomsky: We should act like moral human beings recognizing that what makes us public intellectuals is not superiority in intelligence or special insight, but privileges. There's a reason why people like you and me are called public intellectuals, but not the janitor who cleans the floor; it's a matter of privilege and prestige. I don't think it should exist, but it does. Those that have more privileges have more responsibility, because the privilege grants it to them, and they should use that responsibility to achieve just and moral aims, like everybody should.

Orelus: Well said. One last question, Professor Chomsky. Now we have two presidential candidates that are not different in terms of domestic and foreign policies and ideology. So what does it mean to the future of this country with respect to education, the economy, and social services that need to be much better than they are now?

Chomsky: I don't like either candidate. But I think the Republicans are extremely dangerous. They are an extremist party. They're not a traditional parliamentary party at this point. And the Democrats have moved to the right, filling the vacuum left by the moderate Republicans. So I don't like either of them. There's a lot of good political science work studying their policies. As it turns out, roughly they are about the same. Seventy percent of the population is basically disenfranchised. They have no influence on policy. If they did, the policies would be much more progressive—promoting social justice. But they are basically disenfranchised. As you move up the income ladder, influence grows, and the rich essentially get what they want. That's very antidemocratic. That is one of the things that should be overcome. This is one of the major problems that the country faces.

TWO

Questioning the Essentializing Convenience of Generalizations

Gayatri Chakravorty Spivak Speaks

Orelus: Professor Spivak, before we talk about issues related to "postcolonialism" and neoliberalism, which will be part of the focus of our conversation, would you begin by telling a little bit about yourself, including your experience in the U.S. academy?

Spivak: I was born in Calcutta. My parents were very well educated, and they were anti-casteists. They were wonderful parents. They taught us to scorn the merely rich. We belonged to the middle class. I came to the United States during my second year of graduate school. You asked me how my experience has been in the U.S. academy. It's been actually fairly plain sailing except for the fact that right in the beginning I couldn't get a fellowship because I was not a native speaker.

Also, in the beginning there were no restrictions on sexual harassment. I was in my early years the object of a certain kind of attention from some of the faculty, which I did not enjoy. My own supervisor, Professor Paul De Man, was a wonderful man. I had no problems of any sort with him. He respected my intelligence, and I flourished under his good care. I then became an assistant professor at a very early age at the University of Iowa. I was only twenty-three years old. University of Iowa was a fine place for me because it had a tremendous creative writing program. I was not myself a creative writer. I have never been, but I came to realize that the best students in a theory class were poets, because they were not interested in applying

11

theory, they were simply interested in theorizing, and that was just a wonderful way to deal with the material.

I discovered Jacques Derrida's book *De la Grammatologie* by chance. I didn't know who he was. I ordered one of his books off a catalog and by chance decided to translate it. This changed my life. That was at the beginning of my career. From University of Iowa I moved to the University of Texas at Austin. Later, I moved to Emory University. I then went to Pittsburgh. While I was at Emory I received my first endowed chair.

At Pittsburgh I had the first Andrew W. Mellon professorship that any woman had ever held. I believe it was the first one for English. From Pittsburgh I was invited into Columbia on student demand. That always makes me very happy. I was promoted to university professorship in 2007. I am the first woman of color ever to have been offered that honor in the 246-year history of Columbia University. In a nutshell, that's my life.

Orelus: What does it mean to you to be the first woman of color to ever be granted university professorship at Columbia? And what does it say about the institution itself?

Spivak: Well, it's obvious. It's obvious that it hasn't been open to women of color of excellence like it is with the rest of society. So that's what it tells me.

Orelus: To what extent do you think you may have contributed to a sound understanding of class, race, and gender issues?

Spivak: I don't think I've changed people's views about class, race, and gender because I think I'm seen as a kind of token, as a sort of exceptional person. It is not just here but in my life in general. In fact the class angle is generally ignored because I've taken very left-wing views. That is not a very welcome thing when it comes to actual institutions, but it's certainly tolerated and praised in scholarship. As for the class issue, I am a solid middle-class person. In general, middle-class Indians are from professional families who were colonized by the British and they speak English. We have a different kind of status in the United States. Actually, we are often used to avoid getting people of color who they might feel would be more troublesome. So I don't think my own situation in the U.S. academy has been very much more than that of a token useful to those who have supported me.

Orelus: Interesting. How do you think you may have used your class privilege to effect some types of social change?

Spivak: I don't think I had any particular class privilege. A middle-class person is not exactly a class-privileged person. It's certainly not a class that suffers as the working class does. I haven't really used my class privilege. I was a good student, and I've supported myself since I was seventeen years old. So that's hardly a class privilege. No one sent me abroad. I borrowed money to come abroad. So I don't see that as using my class privilege. Other well-known South Asian intellectuals (though not all), and I won't name them, are generally from a more privileged class than I am. So I don't think I've done anything with my nonexistent class privilege.

Orelus: Professor Spivak, let's talk now about neoliberalism. Some scholars have argued that neoliberalism is a new form of colonialism covered up with a different mask. Would you support that argument?

Spivak: Well, it seems to me that colonialism and neoliberalism are both an entry into the same system of exchange. Under neoliberalism, the postcolonial state's ability to redistribute among its own citizens is hampered. The state begins to operate as a managerial state, managing the interests of capitalist globalization rather than its own citizens. To the extent that the developed countries are better off and the so-called developing countries lose out, neoliberalism certainly shares the very broad structure of colonialism.

But in colonialism of the old kind, that is territorial and secular colonialism, there was an attempt at engaging with the colonized, even if only for ease of governance. Thus you have a certain kind of enabling violation. Neoliberalism does not have that. So it may be worse than colonialism. But I would say the folks who want to do well, to do good, and be benevolent towards developing countries are sort of good imperialists. They actually look at the rest of the world as victims and objects of benevolence. Nonetheless, neoliberalism is worse than territorial colonialism.

Orelus: I just had a conversation with two scholars who have written about colonial and neoliberal issues. They argue that neoliberalism doesn't only emerge from the West but also from developing countries. What do you think of this assertion?

Spivak: Well, capital doesn't have a country. So it doesn't emerge from anywhere. Everybody participates in it. In fact, Robert Reich, the former labor secretary in the Clinton administration, had a wonderful phrase. He called the North in the South the secessionist class. There is a global managerial class in both the North and the South that really operates in terms of this global capital, which does not necessarily "belong" to either the West or the East. But in terms of the structure of the international civil society, the world governance organizations and so on, there is certainly a colonial structure. It's indefinite but it's not indeterminate. It's not run on the basis of nation-states. I think both of the intellectuals are right.

Orelus: How do you understand the effect of U.S. neoliberal agenda on so-called Third World countries, including India?

Spivak: Well, India is competing now. So it's not a particularly good example, though of course everybody has suffered from U.S. neoliberalism. It's not just the United States that has a neoliberal agenda. In fact, if you asked the question that way I would be agreeing with the ruling folks in the U.S. who think that Americanization is globalization. I don't think that the U.S. nation-state has a monopoly on neoliberalization. As you just said, there is a certain kind of collaboration that goes on all over the world. I think it's a much more abstract push of capital itself that has affected all countries.

These days the World Trade Organization, for example, is not as important as it used to be ten or fifteen years ago. Of course according to that organization, what the U.S. should do is impose its domestic laws internationally. If you're thinking about cultural or educational stuff, then, yes, the U.S. is moving into the various countries of the world, the so-called global centers that have actually tried to export U.S. ideology. I must say that the elite in other countries of the world are quite happy to be receiving this. I don't think it's a one-way street.

Orelus: When people talk about neoliberalism, they often refer to the U.S. as if the U.S. is the center of neoliberalism. But we have some countries like China that have had a significant impact on Africa. Should we shift the focus from the U.S. and look at countries that are emerging superpowers, such as China and India?

Spivak: Yeah, people study that. Are you talking about educational, economical, cultural issues?

Orelus: I was referring to the economical aspect of it.

Spivak: Well, more in Ghana and less in Kenya. Africa has many countries, right? So it depends a little bit on how you use that jargon and on how developed the country itself is. I don't have a sense that China is in every country in Africa. I know only about Nigeria, Kenya, and Ghana; and now South Sudan. In Nigeria and Kenya they are there, but there is not yet a particular cultural exchange. They keep to themselves, and they provide employment at a rather low rate of recompense. Nonetheless, they do provide employment.

Some African universities are teaching Chinese language. In Nigeria some universities are starting Asian studies because they feel the Chinese presence, and it needs to be studied. I think it's kind of encouraging to see a rich country coming into generally poor countries with no particular moral agenda, whereas the old-style imperialism generally from Europe would always have a *"we must improve these people"* kind of agenda.

Orelus: Professor Spivak, in many formally colonized countries, such as Algeria and India, we have witnessed the elite in some way reproduce some of the colonial practices of the colonizers. Moreover, the ruling class in these countries have embraced neoliberalism because they are the ones that have benefited from it. In other words, they have benefited from colonialism and they are now embracing neoliberalism, from which they have also benefited. How do you make sense of this phenomenon?

Spivak: Well, it's not a group that embraces neoliberalism. It's a state that embraces neoliberalism. Neoliberalism is not a set of opinions. You have to be able to do something with it. So the state becomes a neoliberal state. The business-industrial complex in that state then takes advantage of the transformation of the economic system. So it is not merely reduced to what you're calling the elite group. In fact, sometimes out of these elite groups you have critiques of neoliberalism. So that's something one has to think about, because what you're calling neoliberalism is not so clear cut. Sometimes neoliberalism is perceived by intelligent people in the so called non-elite groups as a way to get ahead in life, whereas you find criticism of capitalism and so on quite often from the elite groups.

Orelus: To illustrate what I just said, let me take Haiti as an example. After Haiti gained its independence, the same group that led us to our independence felt that they had to be in power after the country was free. This elite group felt that they deserved to be in power. They ended up reproducing the same or similar oppressive colonial measures against the local folks, particularly the poor. I see similarities between this elite group emerging from colonization that have the tendency to embrace neoliberalism because they feel they can benefit from it, and the poor who have been the main victims of neoliberalism.

Spivak: That's true, but I have to ask you not to make generalizations about the elite group or put all of these countries into the same bag before we begin to even think about ways in which this could be redressed. There are tremendous differences between Algeria, India, and Haiti. Haiti was cut off in every way by France and the United States. That was what happened after Haiti gained its independence by means of a magnificent revolution. It's very well documented. It was systematic oppression and exploitation by European countries, particularly France. Haitians gained their independence much earlier than Algeria. Those people are not alive anymore.

Haiti has been exploited by the United States. I could think of countless books and articles that have actually documented this. Haiti has had a much worse deal than either Nigeria or India. In the case of Nigeria and India, one must notice the difference between French colonialism and British colonialism, as did W. E. B. DuBois in his 1925 essay "The Negro Mind Looks Out." You can't compare these people with the Belgians who were much worse than the French and the British in, let's say, the Congo. Joseph Conrad's *Heart of Darkness* is premised on this. These things are so well documented that one can't just make a broad generalization comparing all of these countries simply by the fact that they were colonized.

Certainly, it is true that neoliberalism everywhere increases the gap between the rich and the poor. This is completely true. But I think a generalization about the former elite embracing neoliberalism is not helpful, though the elite classes are full of self-interests and have no interest in the education of the poor. This has been the rule everywhere forever. What do you mean that the elite embraces neoliberalism? What aspect of it exactly do they embrace?

Orelus: I mean they have opened doors of their country to foreign investment for their own interests.

Spivak: It's certainly one aspect of it. But direct foreign investment is happening in Mexico. One hundred percent foreign direct investment law had passed there sometime in the early 1990s. So it's not just that the Mexican government was full of elites. It was that the United States put pressure on the Mexican government. Therefore, it seems to me that the story of the elite having prospered on colonialism and then after colonialism deciding to go with neoliberalism does not fully take into account the specificity of various places.

What happened in Algeria, for example, is not the same as what happened in Mexico in the 1990s. In Algeria, I was working with the socialist women, whom one can call elite. But they were not particularly interested in embracing neoliberalism. India is another example. India is a parliamentary democracy. There are seventeen left parties.

There was vigorous opposition to neoliberalism in 1991, to the country's economic restructuring. The opposition was not coming from the poor; it was coming from within what you're calling the elite.

I think it's more complicated than just simply seeing it as having a good time with the colonizers, and the moment they left, they wanted neoliberalism. I don't think it's quite like that. In fact, by that kind of logic one might say the immigrants are following the colonizing masters after decolonization! That's obviously not correct.

Orelus: As you know, many institutions in the U.S. have been following to a great extent a corporate model of education. Where do you stand on this issue?

Spivak: I stand against it like hundreds and thousands of people.

Orelus: Why don't you like it?

Spivak: Why should universities be following a corporate model? I must first be persuaded that education should be a business.

Orelus: You have written tons of fine scholarly work. Which one of your pieces are you most proud of? Which one do you feel may have had a significant impact on the world?

Spivak: I don't know. I mean certainly there are things that I have enjoyed writing. But I can say nothing about the impact. Since you ask me, I would say I never think of the fact that my writing might have an impact. The one thing that has happened recently because people have told me by chance is that five institutions—I think three in Europe and two in Asia—have begun to change their departmental concerns incorporating Asian studies in their studies after reading my work on "Other Asias."

I think it is a good result but apart from that, I don't know what impact I've had, frankly. I think very little. I'm not very pleased with my writing. I think I have much room to improve. I think I need more scholarship. I enjoy writing. But I already know that there are things wrong with it. I am a very self-critical person, so it's hard for me to answer that question. No, this is not a question for me. I like writing but I'm not attached to my writing quite in that way. I always learn from my mistakes.

Orelus: I recently revisited your piece—"Can the Subaltern Speak?"—and I'm still intrigued by it. Given the new context in which we are living, do you think the Subaltern should speak for himself or herself?

Spivak: The Subaltern does speak. In that essay the Subaltern spoke but nobody listened. That's why the Subaltern can't speak. For example, the woman who hanged herself actually took good care to make sure that people would know that she was not given over to a unique man and that's not why she was killing herself. But nobody actually remembered that message. So that's why I said the Subaltern cannot speak.

Subalterns do indeed resist, not all of them, just as not everyone out of any group is resistant. But when they do, there's often not enough infrastructure for others to recognize that as resistance and respond to what they are resisting to. That's what it meant to say the Subaltern cannot speak. The Subaltern is a position without identity. It's groups that have no access to the structures of welfare, groups that have no access to social mobility. So people attempt to de-Subalternize themselves in many different ways, although some accept subalternity as normal. When they speak through resistance, the real problem is that they are not recognized as resisting, or they are understood to be doing something else.

Orelus: Marxism is one of the areas of your research. Could you share with me what has led you to Marxism?

Spivak: I'm from a Marxist state. I was born in a place with a communist government, intellectual communism. For the first time in thirty years, it's probably going to lose the left majority. It's been a communist state within a parliamentary system for many decades. It was intellectual Marxism that I got when I was growing up—that's what made me a Marxist.

Orelus: In some way, it does. Some orthodox Marxists seem to prioritize class issues over race issues. Where do you stand on that issue?

Spivak: I think those are two different things. I do think racism is bigger than classism. Racism is not just exploitation. Racism is denial of humanity. I don't think there's a competition between race, class, and gender. To some extent one could say also that both capitalists and workers are within reproductive heteronormativity. Likewise, black and white, yellow, red, and brown are within reproductive heteronormativity. Having these kinds of competitions is really useless. What one should do is pay attention to all three and see how they operate, that is, how class is racialized and gendered. Class is important because it works through capital logic and it is also through the social use of capital that one can have a welfare state. We should look at the three things operating together, rather than decide which one deserves more attention.

Orelus: How would you situate class, race, and gender issues in a capitalist society such as the U.S.?

Spivak: It depends very much on education, because in some cases you will find the people who you would think of as upper-class people are not operating racially. Folks who are not white sometimes break into upward class mobility. So they become in some ways racially upward mobile. These things are complex. It seems to me a certain degree of racism, everyday racism, low-grade racism, low-grade sexism keeps the society moving. There is racism outside of the United States. There is a great deal of racism in Asia. I don't see racism so much in Africa, but if you read Mahmood Mamdani's book about race and ethnicity there is a certain degree of what we have to rethink as racism in ethnic conflict.

Race is an English word. We have to rethink racism in terms of deep ethnic conflict on the African scene, for example. It seems to me that by deciding that the United States is guilty of everything, we legitimize by reversal the idea that the United States is the best and brightest. It's not. I don't see a place which is free of the violence of racism and sexism and the operation of class.

Orelus: It has been argued that structurally the capitalist system is sexist. For example, in most impoverished countries people who have been most marginalized are women, especially those who are working in factories. What is your position on this issue?

Spivak: It's not always true. You probably go to the countries you know. What countries are you speaking of?

Orelus: Let's take, for example, Haiti and the Dominican Republic.

Spivak: Those are very small areas of the world. So it's not always true. Think of the whole map of the world and think of Haiti and the Dominican Republic. In what way would we say that they are representative of what happened in the world?

Orelus: Haiti and the Dominican Republic are just an example among hundreds of other countries. We can also take China as an example. When you look at factories in these countries, it's mostly women, young women who labor and are being exploited in these factories.

Spivak: Why is that sexism?

Orelus: Well, because CEOs of these factories have hired women assuming that women are easier to manipulate.

Spivak: But they're giving the women jobs. Why is that sexism? Do you mean they do not rise to become corporate leaders?

Orelus: That's exactly what I mean.

Spivak: I see. Well, that doesn't make capitalism sexist. That makes the capitalist sexist. There is a difference between human beings and the abstract structure of capital. You should certainly fault men, and it is not true that if suddenly they are no longer capitalist, they will then become very kind to women. One must really think these things through. The man who got the Nobel Prize for giving microcredit to women began lending to women first because women had a 94 percent repayment record. So he started giving microcredit to women. And he is certainly not a capitalist. He practices private-sector socialism, so it's more about men and women there rather than about capitalism.

Even within the unions, the labor organizations there is so much sexism that women become permanent casuals. It's not capitalism that's sexist. It's human beings that are sexist. Capitalism moves on its own. The self-determination of capital, especially now with the silicon chip. It's not all related to punching buttons as much as anything else. It works this way because it works with this kind of immense structures of oppression. People who oppress women are in fact not brought into any kind of education that would teach them otherwise.

Let me give you an example that has nothing to do with capitalism. Primo Levi was a Holocaust survivor. When he came out after the war, young people would ask him what were your torturers like because it was intense, incredible torture he endured. This man gave this answer: apart from the exceptional monsters, they were just average men like you and me, badly reared. That was a piece of wisdom that is unbelievable compared to all these generalizations that we have learned.

We make these broad generalizations and write off all people in a group. Education should be able to undo these generalizations. When you say capitalism is sexist then you have to ask, was feudalism not sexist? Then you have to ask, is subsistence farming not sexist? Isn't capitalism, for example, better than the old-fashioned moneylenders? Which is why the World Bank, unfortunately, is able to get into very poor communities because they lend at a better rate than the horrible old moneylenders. It's not helpful to put everything at the door of capitalism. We ourselves of course benefit from it. So I would say that one must have a machinery of judgment, which does not operate in these generalizations.

Orelus: President Obama just finished a trip in Asia. He was recently in India and Indonesia. I would like to know how you see U.S. relations with India and Indonesia.

Spivak: Well, I don't really know what Obama is going to get out of Indonesia. It is true Indonesia has very strong capitalist groups, the Salim group, for example, who might not want to compete with the United States. Perhaps he went to establish economic connections because he's getting beaten at home. As for India, many people that you're calling the elite group were tremendously opposed to the nuclear deal that the United States made with India. But that is in place. It was made during the Bush administration and certainly Obama has done nothing to change it.

As far as economic agreements go, I suppose that India is happily participating in capitalist globalization. I can't talk about India as a whole; it is a place of more than a billion people. But if one equates the country with the state mechanisms, then we are certainly happily operating within capital globalization. I think from that point of view India's relationship with the United States is improving more and more.

On the other hand there is also the fact that India is seen as an ally in the battle against what is seen as militant Islam. We Indians talk about racism, but the 86 percent Hindu majority in India has a very strong structure of prejudice against Muslims. I'm not talking about individuals, but groups. Also, India has a rivalry with Pakistan, which is one of the most problematic and controversial nation-states that are supposedly in alliance with the United States. This alliance is more geopolitical than economic. In the case of this relationship, Indonesia is a little bit different. With the new administration, India's situation has changed for the worse.

Orelus: As a scholar, you don't only theorize about the issues that we have been talking about but you also get involved in grassroots movements. From your firsthand observation, how have you seen U.S. imperialism affect the poor in some "Third World" countries, the ones you have visited?

Spivak: I don't use the phrase "Third World" anymore because there is no such thing anymore. Your entire interview seems to be about United States imperialism. I just don't see the United States as having that kind of hold on the world as a nation-state anymore. The financial crisis has certainly affected the world a great deal but it has also affected the United States so very deeply. The problem is inherent in the capitalist structure.

Where I work among the very poor both in one corner of India and somewhat in Bangladesh, there is more the oppression and exploitation infringed upon the very poor by the local gentry than any remote influence of U.S. imperialism. I would say that one of the things that affected one of the places where I'm most active was the price of oil. That certainly has a U.S. element to it, and I think U.S. military presence probably affects more places than U.S. imperialism. I think U.S. imperialism is more effective on the state level rather than among the very poor in very large countries.

Haiti and the Dominican Republic, the two countries you referred to earlier, are within the sphere of influence of U.S. imperialism much more than the places where I have worked. Latin America is beneath the United States. But in terms of the rest of the world, I am not sure. I think that generalization is not very tenable. In terms of the structure of the oppression that's rampant in most of the states where one goes, U.S. imperialism is a remote effect. You can't point your finger at U.S. imperialism for the ways in which the African poor, the Indian poor, or the very poor in China are living. Where I go near the Laos border, you can't really fault U.S. imperialism directly. I mean that would be too much of a conspiracy theory for me. If one sees how U.S. imperialism operates, it's geopolitical.

Orelus: Although many countries in Africa, for example, gained their independence, we have witnessed many forms of colonial practices recurring, such as the political and economic dependence of these countries on Western colonizing powers, like Great Britain and now the U.S. So should we be talking about a postcolonial era? Or should we argue that there's a new colonialism?

Spivak: That's where you first began. That's your first question.

Orelus: Yes, indeed. I would like you to elaborate on your previous answer, as I feel like I didn't get enough details from you about this issue.

Spivak: Well, I think we should certainly study colonialism and we should certainly see how historically one group of people went over other people's land and took it over and so on. I certainly think we should do that and I don't think anything is to be gained by saying we live in a postcolonial era. It's not that only colonialism is happening again, it's newer structures of subordination, newer structures of oppression, incorporating precolonial patterns into capitalist exploitation. These things have not gone away. And socialism itself crumbled because it never thought of the fact that freedom from oppression does not lead to the desire to build a just society.

As far as I'm concerned, I think that education, true education, and the rearrangement of human desire are a much more important thing than blaming everything on these big movements. To oppose these big movements, win, and then to bring in another kind of state formation might lead to human oppression and exploitation in other ways. I don't think we live in a postcolonial world because we have colonialism again. It's a new kind of structure of oppression. It's the combination of capitalism, racism, and sexism.

So I think I would say that colonialism should be studied with great care and specificity, for there are different kinds of colonialism. I think it would be a good idea if one looked at W. E. B. DuBois's work. He was the greatest sociologist historian of the twentieth century for this part of the world. When he said to Eleanor Roosevelt in the middle of the last century that the UN was replicating the old colonial structures, he was correct. He distinguished between various forms of imperialism, the French, Belgian, and Portuguese colonialism and so on. He was a very smart man. He went into Pan-Africanism with the awareness that different imperialist traditions were not the same.

So I think we ought not fixate on the colonized and the colonizer, national liberalization movement and colonialism, and so on, but look at structure of power without labels, so that it can be seen as shared by national liberation movements themselves. This is what you do when you are actually engaged in a political struggle. That's why after national liberation you don't see places suddenly becoming good. That's a lesson we should remember. It's more about power, capital, race, class, and gender than it is about colonial, postcolonial, U.S. imperialism. Those are big abstractions. I think we really ought to focus more on how one can deal with this human tendency to repeat structures of oppression once freedom from oppression has been supposedly gained.

Orelus: How did Jacques Derrida influence your work or influence you?

Spivak: Well, he influenced me in many ways. I think probably the most important influence is very literal. He was my best teacher, although he never actually taught me. So I think the most important way in which Derrida influenced me was his absolute attention to details. That was one way. Another way is to realize that when you believe you have solved a problem, you need to keep in mind that's just the beginning of the problem. When you solve a problem, it's a plus or minus. The minus makes the plus and the plus made the minus. That's a very tough lesson. That's something I learned from him. It's hard for me to really tabulate his influence because it's a very deep influence.

Orelus: You have published so many outstanding scholarly works. What would you like to be remembered for?

Spivak: I really have no craving for immortality. I really don't. So I don't know how to answer that question. I mean, if anyone remembers me, surely it will be for something that I cannot predict.

THREE

Institutional Racism and White Hegemony

Rodolfo Acuña Speaks

Orelus: All forms of oppression intersect. In your judgment, how do you see these various forms of oppression interconnect? Would you provide some concrete examples to illuminate such a connection?

Acuña: Like Martin Luther King said, injustice anyplace is injustice everywhere. World events and imperialism make that oppression pretty universal. It all comes down to domination and it is hard not to discuss the Palestinian cause along with what is happening to Mexican and Central American immigrants. Race is used to keep that oppression in its place. From there you can go on and on. Right now the privatization of higher education, public education, and the prisons is a good example of interconnection. Also take the lives of the average human being and break it down to its lowest common denominator and you see cases of child abuse, spousal abuse, gender inequality. There is an element of domination and inequality at every level. Carry this to the schools.

Orelus: In what ways and to what degree have U.S. imperialism and white supremacy affected the educational, socioeconomic, and political conditions of Chicanas/os and other minoritized groups here in the United States and abroad?

Acuña: I was once criticized for using the internal colonial model. My reading has informed me and I have learned to digest works on imperialism. When I read Camus I liked him, but I find Frantz Fanon seemed to be speaking to the Chicana/o experience. The colonialization of the oppressed is not only physical but mental and that is what happens to minorities. It is a way to keep the middle class in line and to place them into thinking that at least they have it better than the spics. It is vicious, and there are different levels of oppression.

The problem for Chicanas/os is that until recently there was not an organized corpus of knowledge to fully appreciate that colonial relationship. We're now more fully able to make comparison and draw on the rich literature on African Americans and colonized people throughout the world. Unfortunately Chicana/o and other scholars have not yet discovered a methodology, and they avoid thinking about issues such as neoliberalism that are at the crux of all oppression.

Orelus: What do you think needs to happen in order for social justice to become a reality for historically marginalized groups in society, including those who have been unfairly incarcerated?

Acuña: I am a cynic: nothing will change as long as the present political structure is in place. Social justice necessitates a leveling of society, and as long as the Kochs have billions of dollars to buy people, it won't happen. Life for activists in America and in the world is like Sisyphus rolling that fucking boulder up the hill. We have to understand that incarceration is part of the game. Prisons are big business and big business is rarely fair. In order for prisons to thrive you have to make people "illegal"—that is why undocumented workers are a boon to the prison industry. However, you have to have more clients, so you maintain a decrepit school system that produces prospective clients.

Orelus: You're one of the highly regarded and respected intellectuals who have critically and steadfastly addressed in your scholarly and activist work the conditions of historically subjugated groups in the Americas, particularly Chicanas/os and Mexicans in the United States. In your opinion, what does it mean to be a Chicana/o in the twenty-first century of the United States of America?

Acuña: First being a Chicano means that I have to keep pushing that fucking ball up the hill although it's futile. Second, I don't consider myself an intellectual; I don't have respect for them. They keep on inventing theories when the problems and solutions are obvious. They avoid doing anything about the problems. When I received my Ph.D., my father asked me *si eres doctor que curas?* If you are a doctor, what do you cure? My strategy has always been to take my cause of the moment to the edge of the cliff and be prepared to go over the cliff if necessary. Most so-called intellectuals look at this as irrational—for me it is necessary if I am to remain intellectually honest.

Orelus: Given the level of unemployment and lack of adequate health care and quality education for Mexicans and Mexican Americans, particularly the poor and the undocumented ones, will it be accurate to state that they have been treated as the wretched of the earth, if I may borrow Frantz Fanon's phrase?

Acuña: It is ridiculous and it underscores the futility of doing something through the system. Logically health care should have become one big Medicare system. However, just like the prisons everyone has to get their cut down to the congressmen. Fortunately a goodly number of white people are joining this class, and realizing that they are one paycheck away from being a Mexican and they are the wretched of the earth. Unfortunately, many of them think they are Horatio Alger.

Orelus: Given your expertise and decades of experience dealing with and writing about U.S. imperialism, neocolonialism, institutionalized racism, and white supremacy, what would you propose be done to effectively fight against this matrix of oppression?

Acuña: Educate people and target illusions such as the American Dream and "the illusion of inclusion." Unite with causes around the world. I criticize U.S. imperialism in the Middle East but I also criticize the oppressive role of the religion in oppression that creates an internal colonial mentality. I prefer to judge all religion as oppressive, especially those of the oppressed. Be consistent.

Orelus: What role should public intellectuals play in helping construct a society that is just?

Acuña: Get active and don't act like intellectuals.

Orelus: Let me end this interview with this question: What has sustained you in the struggle against the matrix of oppression mentioned earlier? What would you like to be remembered for?

Acuña: I really don't know. I have tried my best. I hope that others will look after my family; there is no hereafter, but I am still concerned, and my love for them will not cease. I don't believe in god; I am a big boy, so I am not afraid of the dark. But I care. I want people to read my work because without a historical memory we are vulnerable and can be more easily exploited. Much of my work is centered around preserving historical memory. Without a common memory we allow the oppressors to define our reality.

FOUR

Interrogating Class, Racism, and Inequality

Antonia Darder Speaks

Orelus: Let me begin by pointing out that the main focus of the book is social justice. With that said, let me ask you the following question: How has social justice, broadly defined, informed your scholarly and activist work?

Darder: Born a colonized subject of the United States, the conditions and politics of injustice have shaped and influenced my history since before my birth. Hence, the yearning for social justice has occupied a great deal of space in my imagination, personal engagements, political struggles, and my labor as an educator and cultural worker. The question of social justice in all its dimensions, then, has existed as a living narrative and testament of struggle within me, ever since I can remember.

Growing up in poverty and under extremely precarious conditions, it became clear to me early on that some people were very wealthy, while most of the people around me had so little. In school this was also made quite apparent by the stories a few classmates recited about their fun weekends or summer vacations. My life, in contrast, was spent, more times than not, in toil and suffering; caring for others, dodging my mother's furious temper, and vividly daydreaming about a day when I would finally be loved, safe, and free. Such reflective meandering commenced at a very early age and has persisted throughout my life. Perhaps this is why I write poetry, paint, write songs, and dance. In order to counter the ravages of colonization, my soul sought in art a medium by which I might transform the ugliness of personal and societal injustices into beauty.

On the more public side, there were many moments during my engagement with the world that caused me to recognize that justice was a reality that eluded many of us. In school, the Spanish-speaking children were often singled out by teachers and reprimanded or severely punished for speaking our language. I spent many afternoons daydreaming in the hallway or in the cloakroom, as punishment for speaking Spanish.

The clear message transmitted was that Spanish was not only unwelcome at school, but it was considered to be a hindrance to our education and future capacity to survive in the world. Instead of pride for our culture, identity, and language, the children in the barrios of Los Angeles where I grew up were taught, in no uncertain terms, that we should be grateful to learn English, since this would serve as our ticket to a civilized world, away from the contemptible one in which we presently lived. Often, we felt and saw disdain in our teachers' faces when we did not understand a word or could not readily regurgitate the lesson. There seemed to be little pedagogical recognition in our teachers that, in order for us to learn monolingually in English, we had to undergo two steps to every one our English-speaking peers took.

The racialized indifference and neglect of many teachers in the 1950s did not escape us as children. The transparency of hegemony is palpable to the oppressed, whether we have the words or freedom to express it. And as such, we could be aware of the ugly feelings of those moments, but not always able to readily articulate the injustice we and other children like us experienced in our process of schooling. We also saw the differences in the ways in which children who were perceived as being from the dominant culture and class were treated at our schools. These children were often selected for special opportunities or special privileges. They got the best parts in school plays or other events, while the rest of us grappled for the crumbs left over, after the few choice opportunities had been divvied out to the chosen few.

Even worse was hearing repeatedly how our white teachers justified why our same peers were always chosen, if we complained. They were the "good students" or the "good citizens" or the "responsible children." Ergo, we were the heathen, deficient in intellect and character, and uncivilized.

Orelus: For the last three decades or more, you have spoken and written extensively about a wide range of issues, such as capitalism, neoliberalism, racism, and colonialism to which poor working-class people and other historically marginalized groups have been subjected. How do you see your sociopolitical and intellectual activism, including your stance against these forms of oppression mentioned here, connect to social justice?

Darder: As noted earlier, I have lived with class, racialized, and gendered inequalities and exclusions throughout my life as a colonized subject and this *authority of experience,* as bell hooks terms it in *Teaching to Transgress,* has greatly informed my theoretical, political, and practical endeavors. In many respects, my knee-jerk response to all of this from very young was to sincerely believe that a different world was indeed possible—long before this adage became a common slogan. It has been a profoundly soulful belief in the possibility of justice, despite my lived and grounded knowledge and experience in the flesh with oppression, which counterintuitively propelled my artistic, political, and scholarly endeavors for social justice.

So, as would be expected as one matures, increasingly and with greater clarity and substance, the themes of my labor across the board have encompassed and comingled issues of culture, language, power, resistance, struggle, solidarity, empowerment, as well as the dialectic of personal and social transformation. What I am trying to express here is that my very personal experiences with the materiality of oppression, as a known and lived condition throughout my life, has served me well to stave off false and insipid notions of the American Dream, as well as more politically abstracted, ethereal, or erudite absorptions.

Hence, my greatest challenge as an educator, scholar, and cultural worker has not been to amaze my students, comrades, or readers with my intellectual prowess, by positing the most complex or novel or provocative concept of social justice or coining the next new academic term, model, or theory. Such preoccupations represent the very values of a bourgeois intellectualism that has, wittingly or unwittingly, halted many struggles on the ground, through positing interpretations of subaltern lives removed from the people themselves. Instead, my greatest concern has been tied to my capacity to live honestly and coherently an emancipatory praxis, which is principally linked to the experiences of the oppressed class from which I have emerged as a decolonizing scholar. Hence, the authority of my individual and collective experiences as a colonized and economically subjugated cultural being within the United States has served as a fertile foundation for understanding social and material oppression in very deep and

intimate ways—ways that always seem to baffle or perplex more affluent colleagues and comrades.

Perhaps it is for this reason that I have always placed such an overwhelming emphasis on the alliance of theory and practice in my engagement with ideas of social justice, as well as my labor as a teacher,
scholar, public intellectual, artist, and activist. This is to say that my
consciousness and lived practices of social justice, in both the personal
and public spheres, are not simply predicated on idealistic or theoretical notions of society or liberal constructs of humanity or human
rights. Instead, I comprehend, speak, write, teach, and live social justice in radical terms, informed by an anticolonial, anticapitalist, and
antiracist epistemological lens, deeply inspired and shaped by a revolutionary politics and my Boricua sensibilities.

That is to say, I seek to labor consistently in ways that can potentially
unveil and contend with social and material conditions of inequality
and exclusion, as part of a long historical and revolutionary tradition
of struggle in the Caribbean, the U.S., and around the world. Ever
present in this radicalizing epistemology is a persistent political intent
and commitment to the transformation of cultural, ideological, political, and economic structures that perpetuate human suffering and
oppression. This larger struggle for justice then represents for me a
very concrete and sustained endeavor.

Amilcar Cabral wrote in *Revolution in Guinea*, "Always bear in mind
that the people are not fighting for ideas, for the things in anyone's
head. They are fighting to win material benefits, to live better and in
peace, to see their lives go forward, to guarantee the future of their
children." It is precisely this grounded spirit of revolution that most
shapes my praxis of social justice. Hence, whether defined in broad or
specific terms, this revolutionary sensibility and vision of justice un-
swervingly shapes my labor, in both very intimate and public ways.

*Orelus: All forms of oppression intertwine. In your judgment, how do you
see these various forms of oppression noted above intersect? Would you provide some concrete examples to illuminate such a connection?*

Darder: Although I recognize and comprehend the intertwining of oppressions, I neither hierarchize oppression, nor do I ascribe in my
work to the traditional notion of intersectionality that, inadvertently,
renders all forms of oppressions to identities or oppressive social phe-
nomena that equally intersect.

First I acknowledge that my predilection here is profoundly informed
by my political stance as a Socialist and my persistent theoretical alle-

giance to Marxism—warts and all. As a Freirian scholar, I am also keenly linked to a long critical tradition that unambiguously attributes the roots of contemporary oppression to capitalism and its modes of production. Hence, all forms of oppression—both in its most complex and banal formation—are intimately linked to the reproduction and perpetuation of social and material inequalities. Hence, the question of racism for me is not tied to the intractable psychological or genetic aberration of white people (or any dominant culture, for that matter), but rather an enduring historical ideology of race where skin color is employed as signifier of character, ability, and worth of the members of a group. As such, an ideology of race has been utilized conveniently within capitalist society to not only stifle class struggle but to protect and further the unjust interests of the ruling class.

Similarly, I comprehend all forms of oppression as fundamentally tied to a larger hegemonic apparatus of human subjugation, with a clear underlying intent to consolidate and retain unjust and unequal control of the world's wealth and natural resources, including human labor. This has been accomplished through modes of production that alienate us as workers not only from our labor, but also from one another and our world.

Prejudices and commonsensical discriminations conveniently serve to conserve the authoritarian values of the status quo via a well-oiled culture industry that is inscribed not only in the entertainment industrial complex but at every facet of everyday life, including a colonizing educational system, a racializing criminal justice system, expanding prison and military industrial complexes, a deeply stratified labor market, and a free market ethos that perpetuate poverty with impunity. How then can we speak of racialized, gendered, sexual, abled, religious, or any other form of oppression, without engaging the underlying root of that oppression?

It is precisely an absence of engagement with fundamental human concerns tied to social class that prevents colonized and subjugated populations from waging any semblance of class struggle. Instead, individual interests are left to battle it out on a hierarchical scale of contrived meritocracy, conveniently handed down to us, ideologically and ahistorically, through commonsensical capitalist values of unrelenting individualism, competitiveness, meritocracy, consumerism, profit, and so on. Moreover, in the current neoliberal moment, even common historical counterstrategies of political identity have been effectively subjugated and subterfuged by a rampant move to privatize the majority of what were once shared public goods of the people.

Through the wholesale destruction of the safety net and widespread accountability schemes of economic austerity, culturally and economically oppressed populations in the U.S. and abroad are instructed to, once again, pick ourselves up from the bootstraps, without concern for the ever-increasing gap between the rich and the poor. In fact, growing rates of joblessness are touching even the so-called middle class, resulting in more educated people living below the poverty rate than ever in the history of the country.

Similarly, staggering incarceration rates over the last three decades can be correlated with the advent of neoliberal policies and practices that have moved rampant across every sector of the society, including education, health, and social welfare. All this to reiterate that racialized, gendered, sexual, abled, and other forms of societal oppression cannot be fully understood nor transformed, in the absence of a serious political economic analysis of social and material conditions of oppression.

This is essentially what is meant by the concept of capitalism as a totalizing phenomenon, which systematically seeks to control and absorb and usurp all creative dimensions of human life for its own bidding. Of course, this is not to undermine or deny the need for particular theoretical and practical attention to ideologies and structures that both conserve and protect the continuing culture of racism, sexism, class privilege, wealth inequalities, militarism, and so on. What I argue is that ideological and physical manifestations of oppression are, wittingly and unwittingly, enacted, reproduced, and perpetuated alongside power matrices of asymmetrical social relations and institutional configurations that effectively work to both camouflage the destructive impact of capitalist oppression and to promote the social disaffiliation necessary to thwart significant incidences of dissent and mass contestation.

I would be remiss not to note that this perspective directly challenges orthodoxies of race and identity politics. Often those who do not distinguish race and racism mistakenly interpret what I am saying here. The critical theory of racism from which I work engages the totalizing impact of capitalism and, as such, analyzes all forms of societal injustice with respect to their relationship to the reproduction of economic apartheid. This said, racism nor any form of structural oppression cannot be left off the table, in that we cannot understand the complexities of domination, let alone struggle to transform it, without engaging the manner in which different forms of inequalities ultimately support the interests of the wealthy and powerful.

Orelus: From your standpoint, in what ways and to what degree have U.S. capitalism and racism affected the educational, socioeconomic, and political conditions of linguistically and culturally diverse groups here in the United States and abroad?

Darder: Schools and, by association, educators at all levels serve as key socializing agents in the lives of our children. As such, the purposes, interests, and ethos of those who rule the nation are well inscribed in the hidden curriculum of schooling, by way of traditional forms of pedagogy, content, and relational structures of classroom life. Schools are designed to educate students and locate them according to the particular racialized class/caste system of the society. In this sense, U.S. schools have succeeded very well.

Through the commonplace use of a hugely unjust meritocratic system that privileges students who already come to school with greater resources and opportunities, a system of racialized inequalities is consistently reproduced and perpetuated, despite liberal notions of equity or the so-called celebration of diversity. It is not surprising then that when we look at income rates (and in particular poverty rates) today as compared to forty years ago (adjusting for inflation), the rates across the board have changed very little. In fact, unemployment and underemployment rates are higher and more widespread, in an economic climate where many speak of a diminishing "middle class"—which often refers to a phenomenon where workers now earn, proportionately speaking, less money and enjoy fewer benefits than they did forty years ago.

Moreover, when we consider the percentage of people who move out of their original socioeconomic location based on educational success, we find little change, proportionately speaking, despite the common myth that education will guarantee successful working-class students greater social mobility. What I am arguing here is that the educational conditions experienced by culturally and linguistically diverse students are inextricably tied to the fundamental nature of racialized class formation in the U.S. Thus, to repeat again, we cannot fully comprehend the nature and dynamics of racism outside a critique of capitalism and an analysis of social and material conditions of inequality. We exist within a political economic system that requires the impoverishment and containment of a large portion of the population.

In fact, the capitalist mode of production, which is replicated within the context of what Paulo Freire called "banking education," perpetuates, reproduces, and justifies a variety of social exclusions, in the name of the free market, global competition, and national security. I recognize that there are many of my colleagues who would argue that cultural and linguistic racialization is principally tied to mechanisms of white supremacy and that all economic, political, and cultural institutions are structured by an ideology of race or race oppression.

What seems glaringly absent for me in this race-centered analysis is an understanding of how racism functions as an imperative of a political economy that utilizes all forms of social exclusion, including racism, as a means to advance and perpetuate capitalist accumulation, in this country and abroad. What also strikes me is how identity politics or race-centered arguments, unintentionally, have functioned to thwart and undermine significant political economic debates in the last three decades—radical debates that sought to challenge the destructive impact of capitalism on our lives.

As a consequence, neoliberal proponents found themselves easily exerting their destructive ideological force upon an open playing field, where race-based arguments took the "eyes off the prize" and pushed full-on for an explanation of oppression that relied heavily on psychologized notions of white supremacy.

Mind you, I am not saying here in any way or form that racism does not exist. On the contrary, what I am saying is precisely that racism, as a phenomenon of social oppression, has been historically fueled by an ideology of race—an ideology fabricated by the dominant class/culture, to justify a politics of conquest and empire. By establishing a scientific discourse of racialized hierarchy, colonizers justified their commercial enterprises of conquest through slavery, colonization, and genocide.

To perpetuate arguments that treat race as an independent unit of analysis, inadvertently perpetuates a fallacious ideology of color privilege that deceptively categorizes human beings into distinct races—hierarchized by the phenotypical significations of Western anthropologists and psychologists. Moreover, founded on the work of early psychometrists who were hell bent on showing the intellectual inferiority of nonwhite populations (and thus, the superiority of intelligence among whites), the incessant practice of high-stakes testing in education flourished over the last century.

Conveniently, the quantophrenia of Western science is well at work in the current evidence-based rhetoric in education, which supports and reinforces meritocratic practices that reproduce and perpetuate racialized notions of cultural and linguistic deficit. Moreover, the linguistic hegemony of English in the U.S. or so-called modern languages have fostered educational practices of assimilation, which have not only resulted in linguistic genocide worldwide, but dangerously tampered and, in some cases, fully annihilated the cultural knowledge and wisdom of subordinated cultural communities, whose lives continue to reflect the historical legacy of cultural invasion, labor exploitation, and political disempowerment.

Of course the consequence, internationally, has been the extinction of hundreds of languages during the last century, propagated through culturally assimilative practices of mainstream schooling. Language practices of assimilation must also be understood in the context of capitalist schooling, in that the values instilled by the process of hegemonic schooling socialize students into a national identity of allegiance to the state, which promotes both efficiency of production and profit.

The overall value of labor then is attributed with respect to its contribution to the national project of capitalist accumulation. Hence, education in a capitalist state promotes and sustains the racialized interests of its ruling class, who typically own and control the means of production and hence, widely determine the distribution of power and wealth in society. Unfortunately, despite tremendous multicultural and bilingual educational efforts over the last four decades, the cultural landscape of the teaching force and curriculum, along with achievement rates for working-class children of color, remain troubling.

Similarly, there is a need to rethink the early struggles against segregation in the U.S., in that more than fifty years later, many of our children are living in communities and attending schools that are more heavily segregated, not only by skin color but also poverty. All this points to the need for radical educators and cultural workers committed to social justice to critically rethink carefully the project of cultural inclusivity, in ways that fully incorporate the quest for economic democracy in our pursuits toward social justice and human rights, domestically and internationally.

Orelus: What role should public intellectuals, including critical pedagogues, play in helping construct a society that is just?

Darder: This is a difficult question for me, in that often discussions of public intellectuals are fraught with elitist notions of expertise, which betray the very political project of emancipatory and social justice that we claim to embrace within subaltern communities. Perhaps it is important that we define for ourselves what we mean by public intellectuals, in that often some of the most powerful and radical public intellectuals of color I know are those who are most silenced and marginalized within universities and the airwaves. Hence, one of the roles that radical intellectuals of color can play is opening the field for greater communal dialogue within and across communities and working together to create the conditions for self-determination.

In thinking about this question more, there are two quotes that come to mind here. The first is by Frantz Fanon, who said, "Everything can be explained to the people, on the single condition that you want them to understand." And the second quote is by Rosa Luxemburg, "The masses are in reality their own leader, dialectically creating their own development process." In both instances there is a revolutionary sensibility and attitude about the people or the masses that I believe are significant to my response here. I say this in that traditional elitist notion of public intellectuals, these people are considered elite thinkers who tower somehow above and beyond the masses—who should be willing to take on their words but are often considered unable to understand fully their meaning.

In direct contrast to this view of the public intellectual, we as radical educators and cultural workers must strive to cultivate our faith and belief in the capacity of oppressed communities to both understand the conditions of their own lives, as well as be their own leaders and dialectically participate in the process of creating a new world. With respect to pedagogical praxis within classrooms and communities, this calls upon public intellectuals to commit our lives to laboring *with* communities, in ways that allow us to also dialectically teach and learn together in our struggle for social justice.

Moreover, this requires that we recognize the tensions that many of us must navigate daily, whether within universities, schools, institutions, or community organizations, where we are often expected to be the mouthpieces for our communities in ways that reify the very meaning of community itself. Hence, the work of public intellectuals must be understood not as an object that one becomes but rather as a relational process in which we enter with others to share our skills and experiences, in order to name collectively the conditions of our lives and those inequalities that betray our freedom and rights as cultural beings.

As such, radical public intellectuals cannot become alienated or separated from the community, nor see our work as simply that of *interpreting* the world (to borrow from Marx), but rather to *change* it. However, this requires a significant epistemological shift in how we think about our labor as public intellectuals and how we relate both to the people, as well as to the institutions in which we work or that call upon us for our "community expertise." This epistemological shift is predicated on a communal approach in how we comprehend and engage knowledge, as both relational and historical. As such, the individualism and competitiveness that plagues the tradition of public intellectuals and fuels a constant embattlement of petty bickering for supremacy of thought and recognition within the written media and airwaves cannot be what drives the work of radical political intellectuals, lest we fall into the very debilitating ego traps that make us part of the problem within our communities and the larger society.

That said, it seems that one of the most important roles of radical intellectuals is the willingness to be self-reflective, self-vigilant, and simultaneously participatory as a way of life. In so doing, we are able to remain open and supple in our engagement with new ideas and new ways of being, particularly when engaging people who are very intelligent but have not been socialized within the culture of the academy. Often, we witness unfortunate exchanges between individuals who see themselves as spokespeople for their communities, yet are unable to engage with different views posited by community members who come to the collective process with varied histories and experiences.

With that said, this does not mean that radical public intellectuals do not have much to contribute in our public work within communities, social movements, and larger public discourses. One of the most powerful contributions that we can make is to share our experiences, critical lens, and language of possibility in ways that can potentially connect and potentiate working together, toward developing avenues for greater voice and participation in democratic life. In addition, radical public intellectuals have a responsibility to also engage public discourses critically, in order to bring to light alternative readings of the world.

The difficult thing here is learning how to dialectically move between a space of collaboration and participation *and* a space of individual critique, which might require that we speak out against the orthodoxies within communities and social movements in which we participate. In this context, both coherence and courage are required, despite those who might claim that coherence is the only need. Standing alone against those we see as our opponents is far easier than standing alone among those who we consider to be our comrades. Such a feat requires great coherence and commitment, but also much courage to see beyond our frail egos toward the larger revolutionary project we envision.

Our failure to voice our dissent within our workplaces and even among our comrades can often leave us thinking about how things might have been different. For example, I often wonder if history would have taken a different course if scholars of color entering the academy in the 1980s and '90s had not fallen prey to elitist, individualistic, and competitive bourgeois notions of scholarship and had, instead, become radical public intellectuals who used our knowledge and intellectual strengths to genuinely advance an international solidarity movement—one genuinely committed to dismantling the structures of economic and social oppression.

I believe our failure to do so coherently and collectively had real consequences within universities and communities, particularly in light of neoliberalism. Consequently, many educational and social welfare opportunities dwindled, there have been overwhelming losses in worker wages, a diminishing job security, a growing gap between the rich and the poor, record incarceration rates, alongside an unprecedented rise in corporate profits among the powerful and wealthy.

Nevertheless, I continue to believe that critical educators have a role to play in the construction of a more just society, by raising important questions within schools and communities that can move us all to think more deeply about our histories and the world in which we live. And, even more importantly, critical educators as public intellectuals are positioned ideally to work *with* parents and community members to build social movement organizations, as vehicles for collective political transformation.

As the crisis of capitalism intensifies and ethnic demographics shift, new tensions and struggles are bound to surface. Radical public intellectuals, critical pedagogues, and oppressed communities will certainly have to consider carefully our struggles against the matrix of oppression and the ideological center of gravity from which we will launch political critiques, strategies, and solutions for the making of a truly just world—a world where the humanity of all people is respected and the preciousness of all life become truly central to our vision of human evolution on earth.

Orelus: Let me end this interview with this question: What has sustained you in the struggle against the matrix of oppression?

Darder: In the 1970s when I first read Paulo Freire's *Pedagogy of the Oppressed*, one of the elements of his writing that most struck me and that would become a cornerstone of my own scholarship was an un-abashed focus on love as key to our vocation as human beings. I note this because for Freire, all forms of oppression constituted acts of love-lessness. In 1992, I wrote what was to become one of my seminal pieces, "Teaching as an Act of Love." I believe this was the case be-cause it struck a chord within critical educators and students of color at a deep fundamental level, in that the underlying message proposed that we engage love as a powerful dialogical force for political trans-formation and as a decolonizing epistemology—a dialectical frame-work from which we could break through the oppressive structures and practices of hegemonic schooling and society.

As such, my theory and practice over the years has consistently em-braced Freire's (1998) assertion: "I have a right to love and to express my love to the world and to use it as a motivational foundation for struggle." In 2002, I again returned to this theme in *Reinventing Paulo Freire: A Pedagogy of Love* and most recently in *Freire and Education*. Each time my theorizing on the question of love as a political force for transformation has continued to deepen and challenge the loveless-ness that we as working-class educators of color in schools, univer-sities, and communities must face daily—particularly as a woman of color who has had to battle with colonizing patriarchy, racism, and class privilege that has persisted within these institutions and in every aspect of our lives, despite all the diversity rhetoric and multicultural promises.

This of course has challenged us in fierce and unpredictable ways to contend with the hidden structures that perpetuate inequality in our lives and our communities, through our research, scholarship, and teaching. And, in so doing, we continue to move and to deepen peda-gogical visions of social justice, human rights, and economic democra-cy, within schools and the larger society in which we reside.

What has allowed me to survive and thrive has always been that deep sense of justice that has prevailed in my life (which I noted earlier) and that continues to inspire my research, scholarship, teaching, and my everyday relationships. Moreover, through every experience and expression of my life, a deep spiritual process has connected my being and my knowing with the suffering and struggle of others, as I have attempted in community to make sense of a world that was not con-structed for our survival, in that it was not meant for the survival of subaltern populations.

As a working-class woman of color, my thirty years in the academy has been, at times, a nightmare in that I have often been forced to contend with deeply embedded notions and practices of deficit that have demanded of me, and others like me, far more than our more privileged colleagues, yet measured us with the same yardstick. Seldom was there the recognition that the achievements of working-class women of color required from us two or three or four times the amount of work, to receive the same respect and recognition. In the process, I came to realize that working to practice and produce scholarship in the name of justice was not a vocation for the faint of heart. It has required commitment, courage, and coherence, despite moments of utter exhaustion, in order to push against those barriers of civilized oppression, entrenched in a university culture of denial—that wittingly or unwittingly has functioned to stubbornly conserve structures and relationships of inequality, particularly within the arena of research and creative work.

As such, very good people could be so ensconced in commonsensical privilege that they could not help but respond in ways that either demanded our sameness or pushed for our rejection. Hence, paradoxically, it has been through challenging persistently those ideologies and social and material conditions of inequality that we have found the strength to persevere. By embracing a loving spirit of transgression, in defiance of those artificial boundaries erected by racism, patriarchy, and class privilege, many of us found our voice, energy, coherence, and integrity with which to launch a body of *scholarship by the oppressed* that could speak to our lives, without negating the brutal impact that legacies of slavery, colonization, and genocide—seen today in the guise of poverty, miseducation, and incarceration—have had and continue to have on communities of color in this country and around the world.

Thus, my work as an educator, cultural worker, artist, and poet is an act of love, but also of hope—hope that someday we will live in societies that can genuinely embrace the multidimensionality of our humanity, so that our everyday survival will no longer be tenuous or uncertain and our children can truly become equal and respected stewards of the world. It is in this spirit that I also keep in mind that I was never meant to survive, and yet survived; and that so many oppressed people in the world were not meant to survive either, but yet persist.

So I am sustained by the recognition that life is beautiful, that I am fortunate to have a loving family and an enduring community of friends and comrades with whom I share a history of struggle and love. And I also have the powerful example and words of revolutionary women and men who came before and whose words guide and comfort me during difficult moments. One of those is Audre Lorde, who wrote *A Litany for Survival*, which best expresses that soulfulness that has fueled my community labor and my scholarship for more than three decades. It also seems like a wonderful place to end our interview.

> For those of us who live at the shoreline
> standing upon the constant edges of decision
> crucial and alone
> for those of us who cannot indulge
> the passing dreams of choice
> who love in doorways coming and going
> in the hours between dawns
> looking inward and outward
> at once, before and after
> seeking a now that can breed futures
> like bread in our children's mouths
> so their dreams will not reflect
> the death of ours:
>
> For those of us
> who were imprinted with fear
> like a faint line in the center of our foreheads
> learning to be afraid with our mother's milk
> for by this weapon,
> this illusion of some safety to be found
> the heavy-footed hoped, to silence us
> For all of us
> this instant and this triumph,
> We were never meant to survive.
>
> And when the sun rises we are afraid
> it might not remain
> and when the sun sets we are afraid
> it might not rise in the morning
> when our stomachs are full we are afraid
> of indigestion
> when our stomachs are empty we are afraid
> we may never eat again
> when we are loved we are afraid
> love will vanish
> when we are alone we are afraid
> love will never return
> and when we speak we are afraid
> our words will not be heard
> nor welcomed
> but when we are silent
> we are still afraid

So it is better to speak,
remembering
we were never meant to survive.

FIVE

Re-envisioning the Life of Youth in the Age of Western Neoliberalism

Henry A. Giroux Speaks

Orelus: Let me begin by saying that the main focus of the book is social justice. With that said, I would like to ask you the following question: How has social justice informed your work, particularly your work on urban youth?

Giroux: Since the 1980s, youth have endured many hardships, punitive policies, and have had to bear the weight of an increasing number of punishments that are being produced under a neoliberal and carceral system that is really unnecessary and shameful in terms of what it does to young people, especially poor minority youth. So for me the question of social justice really becomes an ethical, political, and moral referent for understanding not only the social costs but also the ideological and structural forces at work under predatory capitalism that have positioned youth, particularly marginalized youth, in ways that are utterly unacceptable and immoral.

In a market-driven society that refuses to make long-term investments in young people, rampant market forces such as privatization, commodification, and deregulation have produced a social order in which youth exist in a liminal condition of uncertainty with few jobs, inadequate health care, soaring debts, and massive poverty. Many find themselves under the jurisdiction of the criminal justice system, attend schools that are modeled after prisons, and too often are the object of indiscriminate police violence. If a country is to be judged ethically and politically by how it treats young people, American politics and the larger social fabric have completely failed that test.

Orelus: In many of your talks focusing on youth culture, you have critically talked about how youth of color and poor white kids have been misrepresented in the mainstream media. From your standpoint, what might have been the agenda behind this misrepresentation?

Giroux: In the last thirty years, we've seen in the United States a move away from a culture of social investment in young people to one in which they are consistently being seen as disposable and excess. They are seen as a problem, particularly young poor minorities of color and low-income white kids. Poor minorities and low-income white youth no longer have any value in a market-driven culture in which they can only be judged as useful consumers. They occupy a society in which they are increasingly being infantilized or even worse, targeted by the police and placed under the jurisdiction of the criminal justice system. The only value that seems to matter in judging the worth of young people is their exchange value.

Young people now inhabit a society in which the pursuit of the common good, social justice, and equality has been replaced by the crude discourse of commerce, the drive for profits, privatization, commodification, and deregulation. But consumer culture does more than turn young people into commodities in order to infantilize them; it also punishes them by criminalizing their behavior in schools, on the streets, and in a range of other public spheres. Hence, we have seen a number of young people being punished in ways that we haven't encountered in the past.

The most vulnerable of that group include young people who are marginalized by class and race. These are kids who, all of a sudden, find themselves in public spheres, such as schools, which become for many social zones of abandonment and terminal exclusion. When you have a country with a history of racial and class discrimination, you increasingly find kids that are being coded in negative ways.

For instance, the culture of blackness is systematically equated to the culture of criminality. In the United States, the market has created a culture of cruelty in which a war on poverty is transformed into a war on the poor; regardless of the circumstances, people are told that the problems they face are the result of individual responsibility. The cure for social issues today is to tell the most vulnerable and victimized elements of society that all they need is to adopt the moral character of the middle class.

Hence, under the regime of neoliberalism, the people who tend to suffer the most are the ones who are punished the most; the most vulnerable and powerless are now told that there are no larger structural problems only private issues and that they have to bear responsibility for their own fate. This is cruel, heartless, and characteristic of a market-driven society in which matters of ethical and social responsibilities are removed from all economic decisions. Those caught up in the apparatus of criminalization tend to be young people, particularly poor minority youth and poor whites. They are the most vulnerable; they tend to suffer the most.

Orelus: So what would you propose be done to challenge the way they have been mistreated in society?

Giroux: A number of things have to be done. One can begin by interrogating the wider neoliberal political and economic framework, and then raising a number of important issues such as recognizing that neoliberal capitalism is not synonymous with a real democracy. In fact, one should argue and make clear the many ways in which neoliberalism destroys democracy whether it is through the production of massive inequities in wealth, power, and income, or through the ongoing militarization of the larger society.

Another important challenge is to debunk the claim that there is no alternative to neoliberalism by dismissing the assertion as both politically false and theoretically inane. This fundamental ideological foundation of casino capitalism has to be unpacked; it has to be interrogated. We have to make it clear that neoliberalism not only separates itself from any kind of political and moral accountability in terms of the power that it wields; it also has no concern whatsoever for the social costs and misery it produces.

Secondly, educators, intellectuals, artists, and other cultural workers need to develop public spheres in which they can provide and help to develop alternative narratives to the material and symbolic modes of oppression in the United States. There is also a need to mobilize social movements capable of making education central to politics itself, which is, using education to get people to think critically and be able to raise their consciousness, make power accountable, and connect private issues to larger public and systemic considerations.

Progressives need to address the educative nature of politics so as to make clear how everyday troubles connect to wider social structures. This means addressing the fact that the symbolic and pedagogical dimensions of struggle have to play a larger role in politics. Domination comes in many forms, and one of the most important is pedagogical in nature; that is, domination also affects matters of identity, desire, and subjectivity, all of which points to the important role it plays regarding the construction of particular agents through pedagogical struggles that embrace the production of ideas, beliefs, and persuasion.

As Stuart Hall once argued, there is no politics without the awakening of consciousness in which people can invest themselves. For politics to become useful, it has to provide points of identification to those groups that are oppressed. Moreover, there is a need to create those critical public spheres where alternative views can be expressed, dialogue is engaged and supported, and a culture of questioning is produced as part of a larger politics of thoughtfulness and disruption.

Third, progressives and the left have to bring together the various isolated groups that organize around single-issue politics. In short, there is a need to develop and mobilize new political formations that assume the power of a vast social movement trying to understand and overcome the lack of unity among diverse and separatist groups addressing a range of often isolated social problems. Opposition must be rooted in a comprehensive understanding and vision of politics. If so, it will be much easier to shift public consciousness and build disruptive social movements.

Fourth, it is important to recognize that any viable notion of politics and change is not going to take place through electoral politics, particularly one entirely controlled by the financial elite. When we talk about the challenge of developing a vast social movement, one major task will be to both rethink the nature and meaning of politics and to develop appropriate strategies and tactics. Electoral politics may have some value at the local levels of power, but real change will only come through direct action, mass movements, the development of long-standing organizations, disruptive social movements, and an ongoing struggle over power.

The only hope for real radical change will come if we develop social movements and a third political party united in their opposition to neoliberal capitalism and willing to engage in direct action of the sort that was used in the civil rights movement of the 1960s or by the most recent Black Lives Matter tactics of stopping traffic, taking over highways and bridges, and holding die-ins in malls, banks, and other sites used by the public.

Power is now so dense and concentrated in the hands of a few people and corporations that they have control of every commanding political, economic, and cultural institution in the United States, including the media, national politics, health care, and the punishing state. We have to find ways to create alternative public spheres to challenge power in ways that are quite confrontational but not violent.

Orelus: In your book entitled Zombie Politics and Culture in the Age of Casino Capitalism, *you made a very powerful statement that I would like to read to you, and I'm hoping that you will comment on it. You state, and I quote, "youth in particular are assaulted by market forces that modify most aspect of their lives." This is a powerful statement, and I would like you to comment on it, if you don't mind.*

Giroux: That comment actually operates through an important series of registers that suggest America's plunge into authoritarianism. For instance, I've argued that the war on youth operates within two modalities. One is the soft war and the other is the hard war. The soft war is basically a war in which young people are both treated as commodities and subject to becoming commodities. The soft war functions largely to turn young people into consumer addicts and in doing so infantilizes them while injects them into a predatory culture of buying and disposing goods and services. This affects everyone, as all youth are constantly being bombarded by commercials and advertising in ways that are quite demeaning and limit their possibilities for being active critical citizens.

The skills that they are learning are really about the skills that involve shopping at the mall, but not about becoming critically literate in ways that would allow them to take command of their lives and learn how to be critical agents capable of making power accountable. The soft war is aimed at redefining how young people think, act, desire, and relate to themselves, others, and the larger society. It is a war in which the only obligation of citizenship is to shop and define one's agency in financial terms associated with material consumption.

In a neoliberal regime of hypercommodification and waste, desire is transformed into the search for instant gratification and is defined by the endless need to consume and dispose of things. In a society of consumers, value is defined as part of the logic of the market, and social relations are reduced to a form of social combat. The soft war is an ideological battle for the hearts, minds, desires, and identities of young people so as to make them amenable to a market that endlessly debases and exploits them. It is also part of an ideological war that privatizes struggle, commodifies public spaces, erases social responsibility from the discourse of politics, saps the foundation of social solidarity, weakens the bonds of social solidarity, and insists on the market's ability to govern all of social life and solve all individual and social problems.

In an era of commodified relations, corporations have access to young people in ways that are unprecedented. Now they can access them through their cell phone, their new technologies, and the new media in ways that completely bypass what we might call parental groups or groups of adults that are usually in a position of responsibility. We've never seen the process of commodification become so intimate and invasive. Disney tries to reach young people who are still in the womb by going to the hospital and giving out pajamas with Disney logos, along with the little caps put on the baby's head as soon as they come out of the womb; that's unbelievable.

The hard war on youth is very different and very ominous as a fundamental lever of what I call the rise of the neoliberal punishing state. The hard war is more serious and dangerous for certain young people and refers to the harshest elements of a growing crime-control complex that increasingly governs poor minority youth through the repressive and disciplinary practices of punishment, surveillance, and control.

The youth targeted by its punitive measures are often young people, especially those viewed as poor, unemployed, marked as racially other, failed consumers, and those who can only afford to live on the margins of a commercial culture of excess that eagerly excludes anybody without money, resources, and leisure time to spare. Or they are youth considered both troublesome and often disposable by virtue of their ethnicity, race, and class.

The imprint of the youth crime-control complex can be traced in the increasingly popular practice of organizing schools through disciplinary practices that subject students to constant surveillance through high-tech security devices while imposing on them harsh and often thoughtless zero-tolerance policies that closely resemble the culture of the criminal justice system. In this instance, poor and minority youth become the object of a new mode of governance based on the crudest forms of disciplinary control.

The hard war bears down most sorely on poor kids, especially black and brown youth, who find themselves in places, like schools and work, characterized by the most severe punishment systems, pedagogical practices, and a lack of resources. We're talking about the

increasing criminalization of student behavior and the ongoing transformation of public spheres that engage in surveillance in ways that
criminalize student behavior.

*Orelus: In the U.S. school system, there's been what they call a zero-tolerance
policy against kids who misbehave. Often those kids have been criminalized
for resisting arbitrary rigid school policies; they have been hurt by social
wrongs at the institutional level, and many have dropped out as a result.
How do you explain such a savage culture of our schools?*

Giroux: Many public schools are being transformed in ways that allow
these kinds of conditions to be produced. Schools are no longer about
educating kids. They are either about training them for the workforce
or making them critically illiterate through an ongoing culture of testing and measurement, a pedagogy of repression, or by criminalizing
their behaviors and putting them in the school-to-prison pipeline. So
the question that has to be raised is: what are the larger forces at work
that have produced this dystopian vision of schooling as either a
workstation for the workplace or a conveyor belt to the criminal justice system?

This is an especially important question in light of the fact that under
the regime of neoliberalism, we have seen the collapse of the social
state, the social contract, and a massive political flight from the notion
of the school as a public good and democratic public sphere. What we
are witnessing are the consequences of the collapse of a social investment in young people and in public spheres that are central to a substantive democracy.

Schools that produce civic literacy, teach students how to be critical
agents, view knowledge as a foundation for personal and social development are considered dangerous and subversive in a country largely
run by religious, political, and economic conservatives. Consequently,
what's left is the emergence of a punishing state in which very rigid
disciplinary practices now become the norm. School is not about
learning but about disciplining youth; hence, it's no surprise that zero-
tolerance policies now define the character of American schooling.

Orelus: In your book, Disposable Youth, *you talk about your experience
growing up as a poor kid in Rhode Island. Specifically, you've said you've
experienced poverty and classism in your schools and your neighborhood.
You went on to say this early experience has shaped your understanding of
class, gender, and race issues as well as the struggle of urban youth trying to
learn and succeed in schools that are often underfunded. So that was in the*

'50s, the '60s. How would you compare the life of kids today to that of those who were born and grew up in the '50s and '60s?

Giroux: I think it's much worse. When I was growing up, the spirit of the great society and the legacy of the New Deal was alive. Young people, however discriminated against, were seen overall as a social investment, and it was recognized that society had a measure of responsibility to make the lives of the next generation better than that of their parents. There was an ongoing recognition that kids basically deserved certain kinds of special priorities. For instance, at the state and federal government levels, it was taken for granted that the state should make an investment in young people because they symbolized the future. And I think the difference between now and then is that we had a future.

We actually thought that things could get better, that there was no going back, that we would get decent jobs, that we would have access to higher education in public education, good-quality public schooling, and that if we were sick we would have some kind of health care. Social relations, based on caring and compassion, were not held up to ridicule. Solidarity mattered just as community, however limited, also mattered. There was a sense of optimism at that historical moment.

I don't think that's true anymore. I think what young people are recognizing today is that the future seems closed to them. They're living with their parents, they're getting college degrees and they can't get jobs. They're talked about as if they're really a problem rather than a crucial social investment. In this foreclosure of the future, in this whittling down of the social state, and in the midst of the ongoing culture of cruelty produced under a politics of austerity, young people have become part of what Zygmunt Bauman has called the zero generation, one with zero hopes, jobs, and a future. In this hyper-market-driven society, there is a poisonous attempt to heap scorn and disdain on any notion of public values, there's no discourse for talking about young people in ways that would subvert or challenge reigning neoliberal ideology.

This ideology of neoliberalism and the punishing state have produced one of two options for many youth: either they become very cynical and blame themselves for the workings of a failed society or they recognize that they are going to have to challenge this system of oppression by getting actively involved in struggles to end the curse of neoliberalism. Certainly, my generation is not going to do it for them because my generation has basically betrayed them.

Orelus: Earlier you mentioned Disney. As you know, Disney is one of the most influential world corporations. It has had such a strong negative influence on the life of kids. What would you suggest that parents, teachers, and concerned citizens do to counter this influence?

Giroux: The first thing that has to be recognized by parents and others is that Disney is a corporation. It's a mega corporation. It's not just simply an innocent form of entertainment. Parents and educators also need to recognize that it's a teaching machine. It engages in a form of public pedagogy, which is enormously commodified and commercialized, and I think it has to be challenged at that level. That's the first issue.

The ideas, values, narratives, and ideology pushed by Disney have to be pedagogically challenged; it has to be seen as part of a larger political project, in which a particular view of childhood, agency, and desire is produced, one that has a long legacy of racism, sexism, and most importantly attempts to turn kids basically into rabid consumers while at the same time whitewashing history of all its contradictions, tensions, and struggles. Unless we take seriously Disney as a teaching machine, we are not going to know really how to address what it does or the ideological damage and political corruption it produces.

Secondly, I think we need to address Disney as a mega corporation like many mega corporations; it has too much power over the commanding institutions of culture. It is a powerful corporate and cultural apparatus that has to be dismantled. It's too powerful; it's too strong. And it exercises too much influence. We need to realize that we now have a mode of sovereignty operating in the United Sates that is like nothing we've ever seen before. I call it authoritarianism with a happy face. Disney is a major corporation that exercises an enormous influence over kids' lives all over the globe.

The corporate club of which Disney is a premier member largely controls the electoral process, the media, and exercises an enormous influence in the political sphere. The game is rigged. Politics is bought by these corporations. They not only have undermined the notion of political sovereignty, they've also become the only game in town that offers opportunities for kids to inhabit a particular kind of subjectivity that might in some way challenge the rule of corporations. What you have here is an economic, political, and pedagogical issue that needs to be addressed.

Orelus: You said that Disney needs to be dismantled. How does one dismantle such a humongous corporation?

Giroux: In the same way that fascism was challenged. In the same way that the Soviet Union was challenged by basically developing grass-roots movements that become so powerful that they topple the state. We have seen such revolution happen in a number of countries, though not all were successful. There is nothing natural about such corporations and there is no reason why in the face of challenges from powerful social movements they cannot be dismantled under a new regime of democracy in which vast inequities in wealth and power no longer exist.

All over the globe people are organizing and refusing to accept the mode of politics that is being framed casino capitalism. In other words, they reject the notion that capitalism and democracy are the same thing. Young people are protesting against state violence, police brutality, and the lack of decent jobs and the prospect of a future without hope.

What such protests are attempting to do is to create a mode of politics that operates within, and is consistent with, a mode of democratic socialism or a mode of radical democracy. That would raise very different questions about what power is, how it should be understood, and how it should be transformed. So the key issue is to begin to raise questions outside of the framing mechanisms used by a dominant order, one that leaves no room for real transformation, except to basically engage in minor reforms.

Minor reforms are no longer acceptable. They are no longer acceptable because power is far too concentrated; the system is broken in democratic terms. The system is corrupt and is in the hands of the financial elite. The system is dysfunctional and it basically serves the interests of the corporate elite, the rich bankers, the hedge fund managers, and the financial class that makes up the 1 percent. Evidence of such corruption is most blatantly obvious in the rulings of a corporate-friendly Supreme Court, and also in the bevy of corporate apostles running in the Republican presidential primary.

Their discourse is basically about serving the rich while at the same time making a claim that it has a populous undertow, which is simply nonsense. You got billionaires now rigging the elections, buying lobbyists, and dismantling social services that mostly benefit young people, the elderly, the poor, and the disabled. This is basically a declaration of war on democracy. These counterrevolutionaries hate democracy. We need to make power and politics visible and we need to think about alternative public spheres to develop the kind of sensibilities and moral values and political subjects that can engage it. Then we need to create social movements that will challenge it.

Orelus: You say reform is not an option. Are you suggesting that what we need is a revolution?

Giroux: Absolutely. You bet I am. But I'm also saying something else. I'm saying that revolution is not a romanticized notion. It's not about changing the White House. Rather it's about engaging in the slow work of educating people to develop alternative modes of understanding, to be critical agents, and to develop social movements leading to social change. This takes time. This demands a long march through rethinking of how we assume our roles as intellectuals. It demands a new understanding of alternative politics and a new way of engaging the new media in ways that we've never thought about before.

Orelus: You are considered one of the world's leading cultural theorists, if not one of the world's leading intellectuals.

Giroux: That's silly.

Orelus: I mean, that's how many people perceive you.

Giroux: But that's inappropriate language. I'm just one of many intellectuals who are dedicated to uprooting a myriad of injustices while trying to revive the possibility of a real democracy. That kind of discourse is generally thrown around very loosely only because I'm older, I've been around a long time, and I write a lot. I think my work is known because I write a lot in both academic and public venues, but being well known is no excuse for throwing around rather carelessly the word brilliant. My real concern is that my work makes a difference. As far as the accolades go, I am really indifferent to that type of discourse. It doesn't go anywhere and has no relationship to what I hold important in my life.

Orelus: To what degree have cultural studies as a discipline contributed to improving the socioeconomic and academic conditions of the less fortunate of the earth?

Giroux: I don't know. There are a number of cultural studies theorists who have been true to Raymond Williams, Stuart Hall, and E. P. Thompson, claiming that we have a responsibility to use academic work to challenge important social issues. I think we should be thankful for that, but I don't see cultural studies having made a major impact on changing the conditions of what Fanon called the wretched of the earth. I think that many people in cultural studies have really made a terrible mistake.

One of the mistakes they made is that they have never taken seriously the emphasis, in early cultural studies, on the importance of pedagogy. And I think by not doing that, they have in some way moved into a difficult, troubling, and obscure academic discourse and terrain, which opens them up to reaching a very small audience and running the risk of becoming irrelevant in very dangerous times. Writing and speaking in ways that might be pushing a certain theoretical discourse forward is fine. But I certainly wouldn't make the claim that they have assumed a role as public intellectuals, who basically should be addressing social problems in the way that Stuart Hall has argued for and did in his own work or in the way that Raymond Williams did. We seem to be lacking those kinds of intellectuals in cultural studies.

Orelus: What is the role or what should be the role of public intellectuals in helping to bridge the academic and resource gap between privileged youth and underprivileged youth, which is getting wider every day in the U.S. school system?

Giroux: The gap is getting wider. I think one of the reasons that gap is getting wider is that youth are missing from the discourse of social struggle. Progressives and leftists focus largely on race, gender, class, ecological destruction, sexual orientation, and the war on women, but rarely ever include in these discourses any concern about the war on youth. Hence, until recently, in the face of police brutality and violence, youth often become the invisible other. Poor minority working-class youth are generally invisible to the left and most progressives.

There's very little understanding of the spheres they inhabit. How can we reach them? How important is pedagogy in dealing with them and in developing alternative institutions? People talk about saving the middle class, but where are young people in the 99 percent? They are not there.

I'll give you one example. Let's take the notion of foster child care. Statistics now suggest that in an overwhelming way young poor kids who are pushed into foster care suffer more violent abuse than they do in the families that were abusing them in the first place. It's an incredible tragedy. We hear stories about these young kids being in foster homes or being in semi-detention centers where their arms are being broken and they are being assaulted; nobody writes about this. Nobody wants to talk about the school-to-prison pipeline—a few educators take up these issues, but they constitute a small minority.

Where are the cultural studies people? Where are the academics working in the universities? Why aren't they in the front line talking about the war on youth, particularly if they take all of the issues that seem to be, in some way, important to such people, whether they're talking about poverty, inequality, or racism? Those issues become all the more prominent when you mediate them through the category of youth because they are more vulnerable.

You can't use the argument that they can pick themselves up by their bootstraps. How can you rationalize the neoliberal focus on individual responsibility as an answer to every social injustice that young people face when children as young as five years old are handcuffed, put in the back of a police car, and pushed into the criminal justice system for violating such a trivial rule as doodling on a desk?

Increasingly, the state criminalizes the behavior of young people, whether it is for driving in the wrong neighborhood, walking while black, or for simply catching the attention of a police stare. Young people have been written out of the discourse of democracy and inserted into the punitive discourse of the punishing state. That is a script we often associate with totalitarianism, not a democracy, and yet it goes unnoticed or unmentioned by progressives.

Orelus: So the question becomes: what does it mean to live in a socially just society?

Giroux: What it means to live in a socially just society is to take seriously the promise of what a substantive democracy means. This means that people should not only be the object of power; they should be able to exercise it. But it also means that you take that society seriously in terms of discourses of freedom, equality, and justice in ways that suggest that you constantly fight for society that can never be just enough.

The issue is not whether we have reached a plateau of justice; rather, the issue is what does it means to recognize that any injustice is really the starting point for political action and that we're never going to find ourselves in a society where injustices are eliminated. That's why the struggle against injustice has to become an ongoing and never-ending discourse, one that is really at the heart and the core of what it means to create a democracy, a radical democracy.

At the same time, you need to create the public spheres and spaces capable of creating the formative cultures that produce citizens who are informed, civically literate, willing to take risks, have a profound sense of the common good, and are more than willing to struggle individually and collectively to keep the spirit of democracy alive.

Orelus: What role should public intellectuals play in helping to build a democratic society?

Giroux: They can play a number of roles. What intellectuals do best is that they make it clear that they don't have all the answers to these problems; they can make us aware of the questions that need to be asked. That's the first thing intellectuals can do. Secondly, they need to build and support public spaces where thoughtful considerations take place, where academics can use their skills and resources in a way that bears down on the most important problems facing society. I think this is very crucial.

Certainly, they need to work in solidarity with others in and outside of the university. At the same time, they can do more than raise questions and provide criticism of authoritarian modes of power; they can help to write progressive policies, work with other critical social movements, and they can also build alliances with other intellectuals both in and outside of the United States. Public intellectuals need to use rigorous theory and critical knowledge in order to address major social problems, while at the same time educating people about the society in which they live, but they have to do so in a vocabulary that is accessible without being watered down theoretically and intellectually. They need to raise the bar of what it means to be an intellectual, but not in a way that is exclusionary. They need to do everything they can to raise questions and help to educate people with the appropriate knowledge, skills, and values that enable them to become more powerfully informed critical agents.

Orelus: On a personal note, reflecting on your professional accomplishments and journey, what are some of the factors you think may have contributed to your success—however you want to define success in this context?

Giroux: I don't know what success means except to say I have tenure and people know about my work. But remember my journey in higher education has not been easy. It was more like a roller-coaster with a number of ups and downs. One of the down moments was being denied tenure at Boston University. Soon afterwards, I got a job at Miami University, where I received an enormous amount of support from a chair and a dean I loved; at the same time, there were people in the department who tried to prevent me from getting full professorship, but the dean of the college ignored them.

At Penn State I think that it's fair to say that even though I had an endowed chair, I had a couple of reactionary deans who I thought were dysfunctional and mean-spirited and basically tried to do everything possible to get me fired. They thought my work was too radical for school of education. It wasn't until the later part of my career, which is now at McMaster University, that I really find myself in a university where I have enormous administrative support and a healthy work environment.

So the question that you raised about what it is that contributed to my success, I think first of all I was lucky historically. I came a long way from the neighborhood in which I grew up, which was in Providence, Rhode Island. I started my academic career at a time when I had access to intellectuals who are really major intellectuals, who now are very difficult to find. In particular, I had access to people like Paulo Freire, Stanley Aronowitz, William Kunstler, and Dick Gregory, all of whom are genuine public intellectuals.

I also started my career when faculty had rights, were actively involved in matters of governance, and embraced an understanding of politics that was as refreshing as it was important. I grew up in the '60s, where there was an enormous emphasis on connecting politics and learning to an interest in social change. So there were models all around me.

I saw the civil right movement unfold. I was privy to various historical narratives and personalities that really helped to change my life. I was a working-class kid. I sought out for working-class intellectuals that I could model myself after, not Ivy League intellectuals. I had no interest in them. I had no interest in ruling-class cultural capital and I had no interest intellectually then in what they had to say.

I'm certainly more flexible today. I was lucky to have and be able to look around and find intellectuals like Angela Davis, Ellen Willis, and many others. These were people I could read and whose courage I could model myself after. So that was very helpful to me. That enabled me in many ways to find people who were doing the kind of work that I wanted to do. Generally, it's been easier for me to work alone because of the fact that I was marginalized. This allowed me to do scholarly work that demanded a lot of intellectual time.

For many years I considered myself in exile. I was not in an urban area; I was basically in places that were rather bleak geographically. That really did offer me time to do the kind of work that I wanted to do, and I produced a lot. You know I have a number of books, which reflect the support I have had for my scholarship over the years. I never allowed myself to constantly write about the same thing.

In addition, I still have friends I can talk to about my work, although their numbers are diminishing because of age and because of illness. My friends have always been very supportive and insightful in terms of providing commentaries about the work I do. All of those things have been helpful to me. I also grew up in a time where jobs were plentiful. So I didn't have to worry about whether I was going to be employed or not. I think if I started my career today at an age where you are starting yours, I think things would have been very different for me.

Orelus: I could sense a deep sense of wisdom and humility in what you just shared with me. I would like to ask you where you have found the strength to produce such an amount of quality work over the years?

Giroux: I grew up in a neighborhood where I saw a lot of suffering. This left a very powerful mark on me because I saw people in those neighborhoods come together and do everything they could to basically address that suffering. I grew up in a period when the social contract was still alive, the social was the organizing unit of my life, rather than the isolated and pumped-up go-it-alone ethic that now drives the country. I also grew up with a lot of outrage.

I think I'm lucky in that I was never interested in narrating myself. That wasn't interesting to me. The notion of celebrity culture never interested me. I mean, even if I tell a personal story, it always has to be linked to a larger social issue or it's not relevant for me. I had models, like Stanley Aronowitz and others, and they were humble. They were concerned about politics; they weren't interviewing themselves. A lot of public intellectuals today that I see are interviewing themselves. They are always on parade.

I had a lot of respect for working-class people who were very intellectual in other ways. I didn't know how to take a car apart, an engine; I couldn't do that. I think intelligence works at many levels, so I never privileged my intelligence over the intelligence of other people, and so I never had a problem talking to people outside of the academy. The academy in general destroys humility and replaces it either with fear and a survivalist ethic or forms of careerism that can produce people who are despicable.

My working-class sensibility provided me with the experiences and tools to deal with a diverse range of people with a sense of respect and humility for how they functioned in the world. Actions mediated by humility and respect saved me from the most sordid elements at work in the university and always kept me connected to the outside world. And I think that saved me. If you're going to be a public intellectual and you don't have a sense of humility and responsibility to others, you are fooling yourself.

Orelus: Drawing on the wealth of experience that you have accumulated over the years, what advice would you give to younger scholars who are working hard to make a difference in the academic world and beyond?

Giroux: They can't and should not ever lose the sense of hope. I think that that's probably the most important thing that can be said here. They have to struggle, because nothing is going to be done overnight. They should work hard, focus, and never lose sight of what they're doing. They should try to do it in collaboration with others because one can never do it alone. They should try to build support in the institution in which they work, and I think they should try to stay humble. They should try to do everything they can to prevent the seduction of power from getting to them.

We're talking about discipline, integrity, building social formations that provide a sense of connection. They have to do everything they can in order not to be alienated and isolated even if that means developing relationships over the net or being friends with people outside their most immediate department. The key to survival in higher education is to have one foot in and one foot out and never give your soul to an institution. You never do that. You have to learn how to say no.

At the same time, it is important to do work that addresses important social issues, touches people's lives in a meaningful way, and uses pedagogical practices that respect students while at the same time challenging many of the commonsense perceptions they often bring to the university. In short, I think young academics need to learn how to work within a larger political narrative.

Orelus: Personally, what would you like to be remembered for?

Giroux: Hopefully, that my teaching, writing, and public interventions made some difference in people's lives. I never expected to change the world. But I did hope that my work would find a certain relevance in which people could read it and learn something and also be inspired and energized to change the world for the better.

SIX

Rethinking Literacy and Schooling in a Capitalist Society

James Paul Gee Speaks

Orelus: Let me begin by saying that the focus of our conversation will be on three major concepts: language, identity, and literacy. The focus of the book itself is on social justice. So I would like to begin our conversation by asking you to what extent do you feel that social justice as a concept has informed your work?

Gee: I think social justice has informed it, although it's not a term I'd use. I think the term is poorly understood. Worse yet, today the right wing has tried hard to define social justice as equivalent to socialism and something that should, at best, to be left to charity. Therefore, the term is contested. To me social justice is about fairness and in that sense it has been central to my work throughout, although my focus changes by what issues are paramount at the times I am writing.

Orelus: Can you say a little bit more about that?

Gee: Today, if you want to try to agitate for social justice it doesn't work by telling people that they ought to be nice or they ought to be tolerant. You've got to talk about issues that are important and pressing to them. Today, I see the biggest issue being inequality, the way in which society in the U.S. and across the world is greatly unequal.

If you want people to believe in social justice, you then have to convince them that equality is good for everybody and that a society that is not socially just is a sick society, a society that is bad for everybody living in it. For example, you can show that countries that have more equality than the United States provide more opportunities to everybody, are economically more productive than less equal societies, and the people in those more equal societies tend to be happier and healthier across the board.

Social justice is not a matter of charity. It's actually a matter of a working and functioning economy and society. This is an empirical matter around which there is strong evidence. Of course, it is also a moral matter. When I first started in education, the issue that energized people was not inequality per se, because actually inequality was less then than it is now. Then it was really all about segregation and issues related to race. But, sadly, even though we've spent decades dealing with the race gap in education, the class gap has passed the race gap for the first time in American history where the kids do worse by class than by race. The society is getting worse for nearly everyone. So if you want to convince people, you have to tie social justice issues to economic and political issues as well.

Orelus: Is that what you mean by social wrongs? In one of your books I just finished reading, you talk about social wrongs, referring to the issues you just mentioned.

Gee: Yeah. I think that social justice is what we owe each other in terms of fairness in a functioning society. In a sense, you and I enter into a contract to be part of a society. Whether we were rich or poor, we wouldn't enter into that contract unless there are certain standards of fairness. And when these standards of fairness are violated in a very serious way, then in a real sense you and I are no longer participating voluntarily in a society as people who count.

We're now being oppressed by that society. It's not wrong to have people with different amounts of wealth within reason. But it's wrong to have a society in which only a small number of people count or participate. When I say wrong, I do mean morally wrong but you really can't convince people on moral arguments alone. It's also wrong in the sense that society doesn't function. It's also wrong in the sense that it's just stupid.

When you have, as we do today, a huge percentage of people without enough wealth or power to truly participate in society, you don't have a democratic society anymore. You have something else. And it's not a society you would have really chosen to live in under these conditions. A healthy society is not only one in which you can participate and count, but one that you have freely chosen to be a member of.

Orelus: Throughout your work you have explored a wide range of issues, such as literacy, language, and identity. How do you see these issues connect to social justice?

Gee: Literacy in any society is really about whether you have the necessary skills, dispositions, and orientations to participate actively in society and now the global world. We have created a two-tiered education system with a two-tiered literacy system in it. Some families' children get basic literacy, which is not enough for them to truly participate and count in society. Other families' children get hugely accelerated, by better schools and massive family resources, so that they can compete almost solely for the good education, for the good jobs. In such a system we are using literacy not as a training ground for citizens, but as a way to exclude people from competing for the top positions in society.

I have argued in my work that as long as you keep arguing for some notion of functional literacy or basic literacy, pretending that some people only need that and other people need higher literacy of some sort, you are actually using literacy as a dividing measure, a sort of measure to keep certain people in their place replicating a social pattern. You are making a bunch of people fit only for low-level, poorly paid service jobs. So that's one problem.

A second problem is with the people who are well educated and have graduated from college, the people who don't just have basic literacy but have higher levels of school-based literacy. The problem with that type of literacy, although it may empower you as a member of society, it tends to make you acquiescent about the status quo in your society. People who get well educated in our system tend to be the people who question the system the least. So, for example, when the Vietnam War was raging, the first people to turn against it were the working class, the less well-educated people. We need not just everybody to get a higher order of literacy but literacy that is in some sense critical and liberating.

Orelus: So what you're saying is that you can be literate and yet you are not contributing much to any type of social change.

Gee: Right. A good example of that would be the way in which the bankers and financiers controlled our economy and allowed it to collapse in 2008. These were highly educated people, and they were highly literate people in the technical sense of the term. They produced nothing of any value. They contributed nothing to society as they brought devastation to it. Many of them knew that this would happen and yet they opposed regulations aimed at preventing the economy from being wrecked because they were making a lot of money from the system.

No one can dispute that they were highly educated. So it's pretty clear that the sort of school success that creates devotion to the status quo of inequality isn't really good for anyone in the long run. What those in power did was devastating. Millions of middle-class people lost their homes, their jobs, and their retirements.

Orelus: What would you say to those who support the theory claiming that in order to have a society that is productive, we need to have people who are literate, that is, knowing how to read and write.

Gee: People do have to be literate, but they have to be a lot more than literate to be productive in society. They have to be able to understand complex systems. They have to be able to engage actively in complex social issues, not just writing and reading and being able to use language to persuade people. In addition, they have to be able to understand the complexity of the world and society. They have to be critical to ask whether the media they're hearing is duping them or not.

But another essential skill they need, if they're not wealthy and powerful, is to be able to protect themselves. You need thinking and learning abilities that will allow you to protect yourself from what powerful corporations and powerful people will do to you in today's world. To me, in a highly unequal society like ours, protecting yourself and your children from being duped is crucial.

Think about this: we go to vote in elections driven by the tremendous wealth of lies people hear. As long as the population can't distinguish facts from fantasy and they can't tell a lie from the truth then they are truly being duped. Our corporations—thanks to weak regulations and strong ties to government—engage in what some have called "legal crime" (deeds that should or used to be criminal, but that are not illegal). Both our corporations and our government engage in constant deceit, as does a good deal of our media. People need to get smart to protect themselves.

Orelus: You would then agree with me that being literate is not and should not be merely reduced to being able to read and write. It also entails being able to critique and read the word along with the world.

Gee: Yes, it is being able to read the world but also to participate in it and to advocate for yourself. Understanding alone won't do it. You have to be able to do stuff that might help you and your family. So you're talking about needing to be pretty smart, well educated, and highly literate if you're talking about critical literacy. Critical literacy doesn't just mean that you engage in political critique and say that all rich people are bad and society is horrible. It means that you actually look at a very complex situation and find ways to feel that you can participate and that you can be an agent that counts.

It isn't enough just to engage and critique, because that's going to leave you a victim of society. One of the reasons I work so much out of school now rather than in school is to examine people's ability to organize on the Internet. People without a lot of wealth but within communities of interest can get together on the Internet and begin to do stuff to educate themselves in ways that are very difficult to do in school with the No Child Left Behind mandates and testing regimes.

By the way, Freire's claim that reading the world—and even a certain sort of writing the world—precedes reading the word is empirically correct based on research on reading and language development. Words, orally and in texts, get their situational (contextually appropriate) meanings from the worlds in which we speak, act, read, and write, not from definitions and other texts alone.

Orelus: In concrete terms, what would you propose be done so students and workers gain the literacy skills that they need to defend themselves in a society that tends to oppress them?

Gee: I would answer that question not in a general way but in terms of our current situation. In America, what we've got now is a society very deeply changing demographically. The American society is browning and the so-called minorities will become the majority. These brown young people will begin to take the jobs as the older white people retire. This is actually very bad for the right wing. You're going to have a multilingual society where the minorities are the majority and they're going to vote.

So it's not surprising that you see the right wing really trying to suppress voting rights, because they actually know that the emerging demographics is against them. That's why you also get all this antibilingual stuff. In California bilinguals outnumber monolinguals, and they are going to vote. The question then becomes: what do I do as a citizen to get ready for these changing demographics? Even if you're a white middle-class person, the question you have to ask yourself is: How can America really get ready not only for the changing demographics but also all the environmental crises we are going to face. All of us have an interest in that. For that to happen, we have to change, we have to advocate; this is a political choice.

As far as school goes, many people say they will try to agitate for incremental change, and they will try to spread it to everybody. In fact, we've done that for years and it doesn't work. We have to change the paradigm of school; we have to utterly change the paradigm of school, and to do that we have to change society's view of what school is about. Because of the current school system, we have essentially produced service workers.

Three-fifths of all the jobs in the country are service workers. You get the basic stuff from No Child Left Behind and then you go and work at Walmart, our biggest employer. If you want to go to a privileged school to get a better job, you can then go to Stanford. The school system is functioning quite well for people who want to make three-fifths of children service workers. You have to ask yourself: Do you want to live in a society where the purpose of most schooling is to produce people to work at Walmart with no real health benefits? Do you think that's actually going to be a good society?

Now if you don't, let's get off the rhetoric that school is about getting jobs—and, sadly, the liberals often buy this line. Schools should be relevant to people's lives; it should not just be about getting jobs. It's got to be about producing citizens for a socially just society. If there are three-fifths of the jobs composed of service workers, how do we then reward them? How do we give those people dignity?

So first of all we have to change the paradigms of school. How do we do that? Well, my best guess is that we do much more relevant learning in school tied to the hard problems our world faces, problems that require deep skills and a great deal of collaboration across different skills to solve. There is a great deal of learning and making (as part of the Maker Movement) going out of school today and we should both tie to this out-of-school learning and mentor young people to actively engage with it to gain deep skills fueled by a passion.

The skills and passions people would pick up in such schools integrated well with out-of-school learning would lead to people whose sense of worth and counting is tied not just to money or status, but also to change and innovation and, yes, social justice. A society in which 1 percent of the people own most of the wealth can't be a good one. Sadly, in America, a tremendous amount of people who are not wealthy still go vote for rightwingers. By doing so they give even more wealth to the corporations and financiers. We have this amazingly sad situation where people who are being shafted by all this inequality actually go out and vote—if they vote at all—for policies that give even more money to the rich.

Orelus: That's the irony. We have witnessed this happen over and over. This has much to do with a lack of critical awareness and consciousness. People who internalize oppression tend to act in ways that are self-defeating.

Gee: Right. I don't think the old-style kind of liberalism that says okay, go out and call everybody a racist and say that we should all be multicultural is going to work. You have to go out and say that this level of inequality is bad for your child; it's bad for everybody. It's going to destroy society and it is not preparing us to really engage with the complex systems, like global warming, casino capitalism, and other such stuff, that will destroy us all. It is wrong to have three-fifths of the people living in society be poorly paid service workers. Society without health care will go broke. Social justice needs to be a reality for everybody across the board.

Orelus: It has been argued that in order to transform the system, a systemic form of oppression such as capitalism has to be critically talked about and brought up in public discourse. Neo-Marxists argue that a collective effort is needed to dismantle it. What do you think? And where should we start?

Gee: I think that's an old-style '60s liberal discourse: capitalism must be dismantled. First of all, capitalism means many different things in many countries. So if you take places like Norway, Denmark, or Sweden, these are essentially capitalist countries that have much more equality than we do. They promote social justice through praxis. They have universal health care. However, they do have a lot of trouble dealing with diversity for various reasons, though they are, in some respects getting better at this (especially Sweden).

We don't know any society in modern times that didn't have markets and still functioned well in the global world. Countries without markets don't function well. The trouble with America is not that we don't have markets, but that they're completely rigged via collusion between corporations and government and monopoly formation in almost all areas.

We don't really have capitalism in the United States. In reality capitalism would be regulated markets that worked fairly and where there was help for people who were harmed by the markets, which is what you have in successful countries like Sweden, Norway, and Finland. So people keep saying the problem with America is capitalism.

First of all, America does not have markets; it has completely rigged monopolies. And it also has no social nets that would ensure that people don't constantly lose in the market. What we have is casino capitalism. We have a thing like a casino where the rich people use money from taxpayers to take risks. And if they win, they take the money. And if they lose, we all bail them out; we pay for it.

Now there are ways to create markets. Take medicine. All over Africa millions of people are dying because they can't get pills, which are very expensive. That isn't due to market; that's due to the fact that there's a monopoly in who gets to make and sell the pills. If the Africans could make the pills themselves competitively and the policies of the United States would allow Americans to buy from them, there would be then some form of equality in international trade. For example, it's illegal for Americans to buy medicine from Canada that's cheaper than our medicine; that's not a market. That's directly the opposite of a free market. If Africa could sell cheaper pills not only would they sell them in Africa but other people would buy them. We don't have a free market.

Orelus: In the statement you have just made, essentially you seem to suggest there is no perfect society, that diverse forms of socioeconomic systems shape nations differently, whether they be capitalist or not.

Gee: What I am saying is it's perfectly possible to get markets to work towards greater equality. Inequality in European countries like Norway, Sweden, and Finland, and others, is very less than in ours. This has much to do with social mobility in these countries; that is, the ability to rise is higher in Europe, in old Europe, than it is in America. So the problem is not markets, the problem is predatory capitalism, casino capitalism. For example, when China at least opened up some markets, all of a sudden many people became middle class.

The same thing happened in India and in Brazil. These markets become predatory when monopolists take them over, like in Mexico. You could become the richest man in the world if I gave you the state's resources. So the problem wasn't the market. The problem was that the market was rigged.

For example, Brazil is making very serious progress towards social justice, but then what happens is that the state begins to privatize stuff and sell it off to rich people at a bargain price. So it's a predatory practice that you want to stop. Now if you want to advocate for a non-market-based society, you would have to give an example of how one would function. I mean, there aren't good examples of them functioning now except Cuba. Cuba actually functions pretty well and has a pretty good health care system—much better than ours.

America has boycotted Cuba for thirty years. If America had not boycotted Cuba, it's quite possible Cuba could have ended up being a good example of a nonmarket-driven society. So it's very hard to tell, because America had usually destroyed anything that would be a good example of socialism. But it's hard to tell.

But again I'll say that many of the European countries, particularly the smaller ones, are good examples of capitalism. We call them socialist countries. They say Norway is socialist. It is not really socialist. It's just that it has a high tax rate and citizens therefore get something when in need. For markets to work there must be a societal commitment to regulation, fairness, real competition, and help to get people back in the game. Our commitment today in the U.S., as far as business goes, is solely raising stock prices in the short term. We do not care about what we make or the employees who make it. But soon there will be so little consumption the whole thing will collapse.

Orelus: What role do you think public intellectuals such as yourself and myself should play in coconstructing a society that is socially just?

Gee: I think the biggest thing is to get out of utopianism that influences people to think that something has to be perfect, because as we argue for perfection, humanity is suffering. Social justice is not a matter of charity, it's a matter of a fair society, and you should invest in it. I happen to do so out of school, but you should invest. You should be showing people cases. A small community or group of people can get together on the Internet and engage in some social justice activity. Encouraging people to participate in what is happening in society might be the biggest contribution you can make.

You and I are not sufficient to make national policy. But we can let the people in power know that social justice is actually a matter of fairness and of creating a good society that will function. And again you won't do that if you call everybody a racist or you say let's get rid of capitalism while you have no example of a nonmarket society. What you want to say is this: "America, you're not a democratic country or a capitalist country. You're an oligarchy run by the rich, and have no free market. You're market free." Now nobody wants totally free markets. What we want are regulated markets so that most people benefit from a social net which if they lose in the market, they can come back, which is what the ideal of America was—at least in the books—but we don't have that now.

Orelus: But I'm still unclear about how can we have a just society when we have corporations basically monopolizing all the wealth?

Gee: You can't. It's very clear that corporations control society, especially when they're monopolies, as most of them are. If you've got a socially unjust society, what's your solution to that? You don't want to get rid of corporations, or nobody would be making pills. Nobody could even distribute pills across the world if you don't have some organized institution to do it.

One of the problems in America is that corporations are treated as individuals. So one of the first things one has to say is: that's ridiculous. Corporations shouldn't count as individuals. The problem is not corporations. It's the stupidity of a court allowing corporations to spend limitless money on ads that spread lies under the guise of free speech.

At this point in the U.S. and world, many corporations are functioning to make society worse for everybody. The reason for this is that these corporations are more and more devoted to short-term stock prices and bets on these and not on making things, employing people, and improving the world. Not only is it unjust, but also repellent. Corporations came out of a time when human beings could not organize on a large scale without having an institution organize things.

Now through social media people can often organize bottom up without an institution. In many areas today we do not need an institution to organize. For example, there's a number of fab labs allowing everyday people to make things for themselves. Thanks to this movement, people in Asia and Africa can build things like tractors, bikes, filters for safer water, and medical tools without going through a corporation; they can do it for themselves. These movements are actually saving millions of lives across the world. People are able to fabricate and make stuff for themselves and others. So they don't have to buy from a big corporation. But they have to make sure that big corporations don't come along and destroy what they build.

Orelus: For example, corporations maximize the profits here in the U.S. They also go to Third World countries where there are almost no regulations. How do you make corporations accountable for their actions?

Gee: The government doesn't control them because they control the government, right?

Orelus: Right.

Gee: Changing that aspect of the United States overnight isn't going to happen. Echoing Raymond Williams, I say the long journey is the real war. The demographics are changing, and new technologies are allowing people to organize and do stuff outside of institutions, corporations, and governments. So the future doesn't look that bad, but you and I are not going to change a government that's already been taken over almost as a coup by the financiers. We can't do that. We're educators. We have to educate people. The message has got to be: it's bad for everybody and there are alternatives.

Orelus: I agree. We need to find ways to make the system work, but unfortunately there are many people that are so greedy to the point where they only care about their own needs. They don't care about others.

Gee: Write about greed. Write about self-interest. Write about how it even undoes the good. Let me give you an example. In Africa, millions of people die because they don't have access to fresh water. I mean millions. Traditionally people have said that we need an NGO; we need a big corporation; we need a water plant. We need these government-run things, and nothing happens because nobody can make a profit out of it. But then some guy uses fab-lab technologies to make a filter for water bottles that will literally filter out anything that goes through the water. He transforms every bad source of water, making it drinkable, and the filter costs a buck. It goes through Africa. Did it change government? No. Did it make it utopia? No. But the guy saved tens of millions of lives.

Think of it. One of the great challenges in Africa today is that the women spend all their time walking miles to get water or firewood. Now that they can get this water nearby, they can go to school or do something else. So that's the sort of intervention that I think is important while we are waiting for major social change. In trying to educate people, let's use the example of people who are actually doing something, even if it's small. Now that water bottle thing is small on one level, but tens of millions of lives is not small.

In India, many people can't farm because they don't have tractors. The tractors are expensive. Obviously it's a monopoly. Imagine a fab lab where they can actually make their own parts to turn a motorcycle into a tractor. Now, they all have tractors. When I look at stuff like that, I think that's good news. The bad news would be if that stuff gets eradicated by corporations. Right now it flies under their radar. One of the things that social activists should do is to help people develop their own ability to make their stuff and use it and be successful.

We have got to stop the rich and powerful from exploiting us. But it's a complex situation. We have to fight locally while educating globally. We need to educate society. We need to be clear that a society full of poorly paid and underemployed service workers is not going to be a good society. We should help people find out where there are local things going on that can be championed and show people the possibility to make a better future. It's all you can do. Beyond that you can't do anything more.

Some academics call for revolution and have everybody else suffer while they wait with their tenure for it to happen. It's just like people who say we should get all the textbooks out of school. I fully agree with that, but then please offer and implement a real alternative, because while we're waiting for the alternative, the textbooks still sit there and de-skill the students, especially the poorer ones. So you have to offer an alternative and not just a critique. And in this case, there are all sorts of alternatives to get rid of textbooks. Champion one of them. Don't just do the critique. Don't just say textbooks are bad.

Champion something specific and positive and real. There are other forces going on, like the demographics change we have discussed and the ever-widening creation and oppression of the poor. In the history of humankind there's a lot of evidence that when the rich go too far in oppressing the poor—and they almost always do—then eventually you get a revolution leading to social change. If America continues to the level of inequality it has now, there will be a revolution.

Orelus: I don't believe that change has to occur only through bloody revolution. There have to be other alternatives to effect social change without going through a revolution costing people's lives.

Gee: That's right. Revolution does happen. I'm not encouraging you to make one. Some argue that there would never be a revolution in America. The point I'm making is that we need to imagine projects to give hope. Corporations wouldn't do it. We need to educate people so they know they are worthy as human beings and that their lives are not defined by money or corporations. If you can get people to partner with one another, pretty soon they can bring down the corporation, but this will not happen tomorrow.

Orelus: That's correct. Where does the work of Paulo Freire fit into this, for example?

Gee: I knew Paulo Freire personally, and he was a great man. It is not enough to repeat Freire. You have to redo Freire for our times. Young intellectuals and academics need to be the Freire of the future, not of the past. He was speaking to a very specific situation. He was wonderful, but we're talking about a new world, a changed world. A world with the Internet and new technologies with real potential for both control and liberation. Remember Freire said we have to read the world first—and even in some sense write it—before we can read and write words with real impact. You have to reimagine Freire in terms of the world today and in new terms. And that's what our job as educators ought to be. To reread and rewrite the world.

II

Overview

Like in the previous section, intellectuals and educators in this section, such as Stuart Hall, uncover interwoven forms of oppression to which oppressed groups from diverse backgrounds have been subjected. Specifically, they point out various ways and the extent to which oppressed groups have received ill treatment in society because of their racial and socioeconomic backgrounds.

Through their analysis, these scholars and educators not only offer clarity on the root causes of "social wrongs" (Gee, 2011), but they also offer alternative ways to battle systemic oppression drawing from personal and professional experiences, which illuminate various forms of social inequity to which historically oppressed groups have been subjected. Their critical analysis denounces and exposes past and present injustices to which these groups have been subjected.

At the same time, they express a deep sense of radical hope for a better future and an equitable society and school system for everyone. They call on educators, particularly social justice educators, teachers, families, and concerned citizens to take a stance helping to improve the human condition and ontological existence of the oppressed.

Educators particularly interviewed for this book argue that if teachers are to take a path toward social justice education, they then need to create and foster an atmosphere in their classrooms where all students feel included regardless of their backgrounds. Acceptance of, and respect for, people's diverse cultural, linguistic, religious, social class, and racial backgrounds constitute a pathway to democratic education.

All in all, this section captures progressive views articulated by prominent intellectuals and progressive educators taking strong critical stances on crucial social justice issues, including the manner in which inequities have limited life chances and opportunities of oppressed groups.

SEVEN

Rethinking Schooling in a Neoliberal Economy

Kevin Kumashiro Speaks

Orelus: Before engaging in the conversation revolved around social justice issues, let me ask you the following question: What got you interested in education and teaching?

Kumashiro: I think I've always felt pulled towards education. Even as a young kid I remember wanting to be a teacher, perhaps because my mother started her career as a teacher. And sure enough, during and after I finished college I got involved in teaching in different ways. I taught pre-K and elementary levels in summer programs, and then middle and high school grades, both in the U.S. and abroad, through the Peace Corps.

After studying curriculum studies and educational policy in grad school, I taught at the college level, but then I left academia for a few years to do some consulting work through the Center for Anti-Oppressive Education, followed by a position with a national association doing trainings for public school employees. I feel fortunate to have had this incredibly wide range of experiences on which to draw as I try to make sense of the challenges in education and how best to address them.

My research interests that emerged from these experiences have fallen in three strands: student diversity and the intersections of race, gender, sexuality, and other markers; the complexities of teaching and preparing teachers to teach towards social justice; and the possibilities for reframing the public debate and making greater strides toward equity and justice through educational reforms and policy change.

Orelus: Would you describe in what ways and to what degree you feel social justice, as both a concept and ideal, has guided your work?

Kumashiro: I'm really drawn to the notion that social justice isn't some kind of ideal end-place where oppression does not exist. Any context that we find ourselves in is going to have oppressive elements and will always be undergoing change. So social justice isn't a state. Social justice is a movement. It's a process of constantly naming and contesting those oppressions and injustices that permeate society, including and especially the ones that have become so commonplace as to be taken for granted and unnoticed.

In fact, this notion that social justice is always in-the-making is what should remind those of us committed to antioppressive activism to always view our own work as necessarily partial and paradoxical. Even our own work, in other words, cannot help but to have oppressive elements permeating it. Every strategy, every pedagogy, every form of activism is going to have strengths and weaknesses. Activism itself needs to be constantly remade.

Orelus: In our school system many of our youth, particularly youth of color, have been pushed to the margins because of the way social structure is set up. The system hasn't provided adequate educational and socioeconomic opportunities to those who are different, specifically historically oppressed groups. The system seems to favor and protect those who are privileged by virtue of their race, sexuality, gender, sexual orientation, social class, or religion. So in what way is your scholarly and activist work connected to the lives of those, for instance minority students, who don't feel that they belong to the school that they go to or they are forced to go to in some cases. Also, to what extent does what you have just beautifully articulated apply to their lives, if at all?

Kumashiro: My earliest work focused on the experiences of Asian American youth as I struggled with questions about how dominant narratives of racism and antiracism either simplistically erased the uniqueness of anti-Asian racism, or insidiously positioned Asian Americans to reinforce racial hierarchies and white supremacy.

I also focused on queer youth of color to examine not only how the multiplicity of racism, sexism, and other "isms" play out differently in different contexts, but also how their intersections raise new insights about the barriers to challenging oppressions. We commonly see, for example, activist spaces that aim to challenge one "ism" even while unintentionally reinforcing other "isms" (as when intentionally challenging racism but unintentionally reinforcing heterosexism), which can be an experience that is especially salient for people who occupy multiple spaces on the margins. Such is why activism must be treated as always partial and paradoxical.

Orelus: Let's look at these issues from an educational perspective. For example, we have now Race to the Top, which is, in my view, a continuation of No Child Left Behind. With Race to the Top, we have witnessed the so-called zero-tolerance policy taking place at many schools serving poor minority students. This policy has been very oppressive to these students and youth of color in general. My questions: How does one make sense of that policy? And how would one compare it to No Child Left Behind?

Kumashiro: Both Republican and Democratic administrations have pushed federal initiatives and policies—including Clinton's Goals 2000 and Bush's No Child Left Behind—that centered on narrow definitions of standards and accountability that relied on rhetorical, not research-based, backing for increased student testing with high stakes. This over- and mis-use of testing has taken on new life today in the current proliferation of state legislation to incentivize teaching with "merit pay" that rewards teachers for raising test scores, as if the problem is merely that too many teachers are lazy and incompetent.

This heightened focus on holding individuals (individual students, individual educators) accountable emerges from the more fundamental assumption that the competition of a marketplace will drive improvement: like grocery stores in a neighborhood, it's the competition that will incentivize innovation, effort, and success. Over the past few decades, and despite research to the contrary, neoliberalism and its insistence that systems will improve when they are marketized have become the "common sense" of not only economic, but also educational reforms.

Race to the Top continues this neoliberal framing by incentivizing competition among schools (by supporting charter expansion) and even between states (by shifting formula grants to competitive grants). Such a framing individualizes the problem. What is problematic here is the implication that schools are failing, and that this failure is because individual students, teachers, principals, schools, and states are not trying hard enough. When we scapegoat individuals, we mask the systemic nature of the problems we face.

Orelus: Right. It seems to me reform doesn't seem to be the solution to the problems we have been facing. Should we call then for a revolution of the system or should we continue reforming it with the hope it will serve the needs of all people, regardless of their race, gender, sexuality, social class, and of course, language?

Kumashiro: I definitely think that major changes are needed with public education. However, I do not think that we can take the so-called "reforms" that are under way right now and try to tinker with them. Rather, I think that we need very different kinds of reforms. And to start, we need to think differently about the very purposes and goals of education. Sometimes people say that the "achievement gaps" (the gaps in test scores between, on the one hand, White and Asian American students, and on the other, all other groups of color: African American, Latino/a, Native American, and Pacific Islander) are signs that the school systems are failing to achieve the commonly expressed goals of leveling the playing fields, preparing all students to succeed, and providing equal education opportunity.

History reminds us, however, that such have not always been the goals of public education: we created the earliest schools for only certain groups, and as we were forced to integrate more and more people, we came up with more ways to sort them, as through segregation or tracking. Schools have always served primarily a sorting function in our nation, as they have and continue to do in societies throughout the world where schooling serves primarily to socialize into existing structures and hierarchies, with academics and job preparation in the service of that larger goal.

The achievement gap is not necessarily a sign that schools are failing, but is actually a sign that schools are succeeding in doing exactly what they were set up to do. So when we talk about education, we should not be talking about how we return to some better past or how we can tinker with the system and think that it's going to accomplish something different. We need to fundamentally rethink what role education is supposed to be playing in a democratic society.

To do so, we need to be asking different kinds of questions. For example, rather than asking how we close the gap, we need to be asking how to better acknowledge and grapple with historic patterns that we really haven't addressed, like segregated schools and our continued reliance on students' residence to determine school assignment.

We need to be asking how to better address structured inequities, like funding formulas in which local property values and community wealth overdetermine school funding. We need to be asking who is making decisions about school reforms, and why is it that corporations and wealthy individuals and venture philanthropists can have unprecedented and unchecked influence on policies and practices, like what the curriculum looks like or what assessment looks like? If we were to truly address structural and systemic problems and not try to individualize the problem by measuring/punishing/fixing individual teachers, or individual principals, or individual schools, then we would be seeing, as you put it, a revolution in education.

Orelus: Schools are part of the fabric of society, so what's happening at the school level is a reflection of what's happening in society at large. Would you agree to effect social change at the school level, we need to start by changing the economic and political structure that leads to what's been happening at the school? In other words, do you think that some kind of social change is needed to occur at a sociopolitical level in order for schools to be transformed in ways that would benefit students regardless of their background?

Kumashiro: Yes, I absolutely agree with you. Schools are not merely a microcosm or reflection of society; schools are integral components of society, they are a part of it, which means that anything that permeates society is going to permeate schools as well. For example, racism is an everyday fixture of our nation and our society; it permeates our lives at the various individual, institutional, and ideological levels, and therefore it's going to permeate schools at varying levels as well. I think that a lot of the problems with schools, as you're pointing out, are intimately tied to other institutions and societal structures.

We cannot address school segregation and racial divides unless we also address housing segregation and community wellness. We cannot address inadequate funding and resources in schools unless we also address the broader disinvestment in certain communities, including policies and practices that exacerbate the wealth gap, widespread poverty, inadequate access to health care and social services, and other changes that make the public sector less publicly funded. Transforming education, as Paulo Freire argued, requires that we raise our awareness of these broader systemic problems, and that we premise learning about the world on our acting to change it.

Orelus: Absolutely, absolutely. Let me ask you a question that has two components. Let me begin with the first one: In your imagination, what would it look like to live in an equitable and socially just society?

Kumashiro: As I pointed out earlier, I think a socially just society is not one where there are no injustices and biases and oppressions. I think a socially just society is a society that is both committed to naming and addressing the injustices that exist and is acting on that commitment in antioppressive ways. I make similar arguments about antioppressive education: a socially just school is one that positions teaching and learning to be in the service of justice, which means that we ask troubling questions about what we do not yet know and what we think we already do know, and we allow the paradoxes and partialities that arise to be at the heart of what we do.

As I mentioned at the start of this interview, the necessarily paradoxical nature of antioppressive activism is precisely what opens rather than closes off the potential of our work to be transformative, and it is this opening that creates significant resources that schools can leverage towards social justice.

Orelus: Now here is the second component of the question: What role do you think public intellectuals should play in cobuilding a socially just society?

Kumashiro: I think that's such a great question, particularly for those of us in higher education, who often are rightfully critiqued for working in an "ivory tower" that is disconnected from and unaccountable to our communities. We have not yet, as a profession, realized the impact that we can have when we view our work as being in solidarity with communities that struggle the most. One of my mentors, the late Eric Rofes, argued that academia is an assimilationist profession, in which we place most value on journal articles and on talking to ourselves, rather than leveraging our research to impact policy and practice. We need to redefine what it means to be in academia: in addition to changing the field of research, we should also be public intellectuals, grassroots organizers, collaborators with schools and communities, and/or workers committed to raising public awareness and changing educational practices.

So often we think about social justice activism very narrowly, as in, let's engage in some kind of an action (a protest, a rally) that leads to some kind of a change in law or policy. Such actions and changes are important, but they need to be seen as part of something bigger. What changes societies are social movements.

Take, for example, the civil rights movement, which some people associate with such legislative and litigative victories as the Civil Rights Act of 1964 or Brown versus Board of Education in 1954. These were indeed historic, but even leaders and activists at the time were arguing that they were compromises, they were steps forward but also steps back. It's not the case that the civil rights movement is defined primarily by changes in law and policy.

Also significant was that the civil rights movement shifted the public consciousness. It changed how we, as a nation, thought and talked about things like race and rights and democracy and diversity. Same with the Occupy movement: it didn't lead to any major changes in law at the time when it was happening, but what was significant was that it made household language such politicized concepts as the 1 percent and the 99 percent, or the masses and the elite.

We do need to change policies and we do need to change practices, but we also need to change how we think and talk about the very purposes and promises of public education in a democratic society. Academics and educators should be striving to have impact far beyond our journals, and even far beyond our classrooms. We need to be leveraging our resources and collectivizing as educators and researchers to raise public awareness, reframe public debates, and reclaim public education as a central site of movement building towards equity and justice.

EIGHT

Redefining Blackness in the Twenty-First Century

Molefi Kete Asante Speaks

Orelus: How do you think social justice has informed your work?

Asante: My passion is for a word that encompasses your idea of social justice but is found in the classical African language of *ciKam*, the language of Kemet. That word is *Maat,* and it is translated in English by truth, righteousness, justice, harmony, balance, order, and reciprocity. Consequently, I am not only interested in what people call *social justice*, which is essentially equality and fairness, but I am also interested in what the ancient Africans would probably refer to as restorative justice with an aspect of economic justice as well.

There is a story that is often told about the Nile River. When it overflowed, officials had the big problem of trying to figure out how much land people had prior to the flood and where that land would be and how they would go about actually repairing the damage that has been done by the inundation. So they came up with this term called *serudja-ta*. This concept of *serudja-ta* means repairing and restoring. So it was not simply that you would repair but that you would also restore people to their former position

When you look at what's happened to African people, particularly in the Western world, the notion of treating others with some degree of equality does not really get to the idea of restoring us to the position from which we have lost so much. You have to have something that's a little deeper than simply treating people equally, because this is where reparations would come in, for example. You have to restore and repair, and that is in part what I focus on in my own work.

Orelus: Do you feel that we have achieved some of that by having Obama as the first black president?

Asante: The fact that Obama is the first president of African origin shows us a way forward. But it does not really mean that we ought to rest in this place, because there are a couple of problems with the Obama presidency. One of them is that the majority of white people did not vote for Obama in either 2008 or 2012. We have not crossed the river to be at a position where we can say we are surely within an era of white people willing to vote in a majority for a black candidate. That didn't happen.

We still know that McCain got the majority of the white vote in the first Obama election and Romney got the majority of the white vote in the second. So that's one problem with Obama's election. It is also the source of many of the problems he confronted during both administrations.

The second issue is that Obama's election marginalizes the African and Latino communities in the sense that white people assume that they had basically done something that they had not totally done; that is, that whites had done something for Latinos, Blacks, and Asians. The truth is that whites felt like *they* had done something worthwhile when Obama was elected; that is, they had taken off the table the discussion about racism and white privilege.

This false belief, a consciousness of mythic illusion, crippled the Obama administrations because whites acted as if they had given Obama leadership of the country. They felt that the election of Obama was seen basically as something that was *given* to the black community or to the Mexican, Puerto Rican, or Asian communities. Initially many whites wrapped themselves in the clothes of compassion because Obama's elections showed that white people were more liberal than they actually were in the American electorate. White supremacy emerged when whites accepted the myth that they had granted a black man something they did not grant, the presidency.

Orelus: I will return to the Obama presidency later. Let me ask you the following question. For the last forty years or more, you have written extensively about Afrocentrism and, of course, racism. How do you see those terms connect to social justice?

Asante: First of all, let me just say that what I have written about is Afrocentricity. I rarely use the word Afrocentrism because Afrocentrism was first used by the opponents of Afrocentricity because they saw it as religion. It's not a religion. But how do these terms connect to social justice? Fundamentally, Afrocentricity, which is of course the basic philosophical context out of which I work, suggests that African people must be viewed and must view themselves as centered, as subjects in our own narratives.

In other words, we are not spectators to Europe, and we are not on the periphery of Europe just looking in but we are actors; we're historical figures. We have achieved; we do achieve; we have failed but we did win victories, and we have suffered. We have been very successful in many ways. So for an African person, a person of African descent, it's essential that we don't view ourselves as being imitations of Europeans.

We must see ourselves as being subjects of our own historical experiences and must abandon Eurocentrism in our brain. Mental bondage can be almost as terrible as physical bondage. It is the inability to escape the brutal hold that the ancestors of our oppressors continue to hold on our brains in terms of religion, media, ethics, education, and social and economic values. Yet we know that there's nothing more significant for us than to understand and appreciate our own historical roles. So that's the place of Afrocentricity.

Pan-Africanism comes from the idea that we believe that collectively from the last five hundred years people of African descent have basically suffered from the same type of oppression at the hands of Europe. Whether it is on the continent of Africa, in America, or in the Caribbean, we have had the same collective experience. It may have been different in degrees, but there are great similarities in responses to the historical challenges of African populations.

European interventions and kidnappings led to the redistribution by force of African populations. Thus, the need to focus on Pan-Africanism as an important objective is paramount but it is not the same as Afrocentricity. Where Pan-Africanism is a destination, Afrocentricity is the train barreling toward Pan-Africanism. African people need to recognize these similarities so they are able to operate and organize on an international, transcontinental level in order to be able to not only advance African culture but also to promote the unity of Africa itself as a continental state.

In addition, this means that we seek the restoration of Africa's sense of identity and purpose. We see racism as a system, and we see this system particularly as operating in the West as one that celebrates white privilege and advantage. This is why white police have been able to kill black people without being convicted of a crime. Not only does racism celebrate white privilege but it also protects white privilege by laws, rules, and de facto practices of white protection.

My work argues that the fundamental aspect of racism in the Western world is really one that I call Westernity, because it is a combination of many attributes of white domination in media, religion, and education. Westernity is a combination of the four pillars of *imperialism, neoliberalism, colonialism,* and what I call *conceptual aggression.* The elements are related to white supremacy and white control of ideas not by virtue but by propaganda and bluff.

This is one of the things I have dealt with mostly in my work as an African and as a student of African culture and philosophy. We have to deal with this question of conceptual aggression where white people basically want to claim everything. Essentially this is the projection of Europe and America's idea of science, art, history, and philosophy as being derived from Greece.

Of course, this is not simply wrong; it is the origin of the West's arrogance. Those who study history know that the African continent is not merely the original home of human beings but the earliest home of civilization in terms of organizing of communities, naming of things, and the revolutionary ideas of geometry, mathematics, medicine, art, philosophy, and architecture. Yet the promotion of Eurocentric ideas as exceptional and universal is a serious problem of arrogance of ethnicity, possibly we can say ethnocentrism.

Universalism is really a restricted term to Eurocentric particularism. That the particular European experience is basically expanded and enlarged to be universalism is deeply flawed and problematic. There is this idea that what is correct for Europe is basically the right thing for everyone, whether it is the discussion of dignity, justice, or a discussion of almost any concept.

Let me be clear, there are some Western ideas that might now be global, but that is different from calling the Western ideas universal; global in a geographic sense speaks to the extent of influence, but to claim that a particular culture is universal is much too sanctimonious. Whatever the concept might be, Europe becomes the standard and the norm, and that of course is fundamentally at odds with Afrocentricity.

My argument is that the human cultural table is quite large and Europe cannot assume all the space.

Orelus: Okay, thank you so much for clarifying, specifically for making the distinction between Afrocentrism and Afrocentricity. You have written about Africa and you have traveled to the continent quite often. To what extent do you think Western imperialism has impacted the social, social economic, and cultural conditions of Africans?

Asante: It is has thoroughly contaminated African ideas, religion, and social relations. It has thoroughly contaminated Africans' view of themselves. It has thoroughly rewritten Africa's history in the image of Europe. By this I mean that immense and unbridled greed has been unleashed on the African world, with untold examples of brutality, theft, and corruption, whether it is in the search for gold, diamonds, uranium, or even the more modern search for the technological minerals in the Democratic Republic of the Congo for the technological transformation of the Western world today. All of these things have affected a struggling Africa trying to find its own place, its own center after five hundred years and more of interventions.

There will be some successes, but there are many failures linked to economic, educational, and political effects of Western imperialism on people in the continent of Africa. It has been devastating. Mental enslavement is everywhere. There are Africans living in the continent who whiten or try to whiten their skin by using skin lighteners. They also try to straighten their hair; they want to do all of these things because of what the West brought to Africa. What Westernity brought to Africa was the idea that Africa was inferior and that Europe was somehow superior.

So people are trying to become like Europeans, and that is very crippling because it speaks to the depth of self-hatred. Even in a country with such clear revolutionary politics as Zimbabwe you cannot ride an intercity bus, say from Harare to Bulawayo, without being bombarded by the four or five hours of Christian or European gratuitous propaganda by whites. There is no law against it, but there should be a public outcry against it. Like the students who pulled down the statue of the racist Cecil John Rhodes at the University of Cape Town, other students and African masses must pull out the conceptual arrows of white propaganda from their brains. This will take time.

Orelus: This has a lot to do with the legacy of colonialism, which has impacted people of African descent who sadly believe that the whiter the better and that whatever Western is better. We need to find ways to decolonialize our mind.

Asante: Education, as we know it, is probably not a remedy for that, as it accommodates the current economic needs of the Western world. We need to initiate a better way to transmit values to our young people. We need to dare to dream for a better system, because if you have an educational system in a racist society, it will produce a racist educational system. Likewise, if you have a Marxist political system, you will have a Marxist education system.

What we really need in the Western world is a radical change. We have this plural society with different cultural centers, and we have this tremendous amount of energy on the part of African people and Latin people everywhere. We need a revolutionary aspect to modern education. And I don't think that's going to be in some multicultural character that Diane Ravitch talks about where you basically have Europeans at the top and everybody else under the wings of Europe. We have to design an educational system that will arrest the greediest form of white supremacy and intervene to keep it from occupying all kinds of space—the conceptual space, the economic space, and the academic space. Such an action is a genuine revolutionary process.

Orelus: Indeed. I would like to go back to the term social justice. *What do you think needs to happen in order for the term* social justice *to become a reality for marginalized groups, such as African Americans, Blacks, Latinos, and Asians, among other minorities?*

Asante: I've thought about this a lot. In order for that to happen, we cannot crush the dreams of the oppressed people without consequences. The human spirit always looks to freedom, and I think that is a human story. So whether we are in the Americas or on the continent of Africa, as Africans we are confronted with the challenges of white obstacles, or as Michael Tillotson calls them, agency reduction formations, which seek to prevent Africans from advancing a common narrative.

The best principles of equality, human rights, and human dignity only emerge in a society like this one where we have to struggle for these rights. We have to constantly struggle because inequality is enshrined in the American body politic as initial birthright contradictions. The only way you can deal with these contradictions is to keep struggling against them. You may convince one generation, and then forty years later you have to convince another one of the same thing, because the generative power of the institution that exists in the society keeps creating over and over again the same type of people and the same type of prejudices and the same types of privileges.

You have to fight against them every generation. They don't go away because institutions won't go away. So what can we do? What must we do? We must continue to fight; we must stretch the basis for proper distribution of resources. We must continue to try to overcome all forms of oppression and discrimination. These are the keys to the advancement of society. Anyway, all forms of justice—ecological, atmospheric, spatial, and geographic—are ultimately social because they involve human beings. That is why I speak of the advancement of society.

Orelus: You are one of the top world leading intellectuals who has critically and steadfastly talked and written about the living conditions of blacks and brown people in the Americas and Africa. In your opinion, what does it mean to be black in the twenty-first century?

Asante: To be black is not just a color. For me, to be black first means that I stand against all forms of oppression. Blackness is a value of antiracism; it is a positive advance for humans to declare that they are black because it means they see the overwhelming power of resistance to evil, criminal behavior, and rampant racism. It is a Charlie Hebdo moment to say that I am black or you are black regardless to your complexion. Of course, there is a historical narrative to blackness, but at the core of that narrative itself is the humanity of being against all forms of injustice. To me, that is the meaning of the blackest blackness.

Moreover, blackness represents a challenge to every form of irrationality and ignorance. To be black is advancement for justice. If you say, "I'm black," the connotation is that you are a person who fights to advance justice. To be black is a call for solidarity with truth. It's a recognition of identity similarities and sameness with those who are fighting various forms of oppression. To me, that's what it is to be black. It is, in that sense, a moral position. It's an ethical trust into the fog of ignorance and injustice.

Orelus: Given the level of unemployment and lack of adequate health care and quality education that black and brown people are experiencing in the Americas, would it be fair to say that black and brown people are facing a new form of racism?

Asante: I would say no; it's the same white privilege. It's not necessarily a new form of racism. Racism is like a chameleon that changes colors depending on its environment. It's the same racism that is expressed in all its variations. People may have changed. We may have more brown people now than we had before, but they continue to experience racism.

The Pew Charitable Trust's recent studies about Asian Americans brought out a lot of Asians to say: "Hey, wait a minute, you do the study but you don't realize how much racism Asians have faced. We have to constantly push for justice in all of its forms." If you look at the conditions of the African American community, for example, in terms of employment, housing stock, transportation opportunities, education levels, incarceration without education and rehabilitation, and health care, there's no way you can say that the United Sates is a first-rate country.

Orelus: When you think of the increasing number of black and brown people being incarcerated in the United States, one must ask if we are not living in a new form of Jim Crow.

Asante: Definitely. In fact, Michael Tillotson and Michelle Alexander wrote *Invisible Jim Crow* and *The New Jim Crow*, respectively. Michelle Alexander is talking more about incarceration, but Tillotson is talking about the invisible structures that remain in place for the prisoner once he is released. If it was true that a week before the Civil War black people owned about 1 percent of the land in the U.S., and if it's still true now that we own about 4 percent, you have to ask what has happened? I mean, why is it that African people have not made greater gains in the society?

The answer is very simple. The lending structures of the banks, the economic predators, and the greed have really eaten up many of the resources of the African American community. There's not only the theft of the land and the property, but it's a theft of the people themselves, theft of ideas, and theft of concepts. It's a total theft. Capitalism is a system that is so dangerous that you have to be careful, because ideas we have may also be eaten up by it. They have basically taken everything, and this theft of course is the very beginning of Westernity, particularly with the whole British seventeenth-century idea of going around the world trying to steal the Spanish gold.

The whole system was based on this idea of the British government setting up these pirates, licensing them, and calling them privateers so they could go around stealing the Spanish gold by attacking Spanish ships. But the Spanish themselves had already begun this process of theft and thievery not just of ideas but also of the gold and the resources of people in Latin America and other parts of the world. So we're living in a whole world view of thievery where greed itself is fundamental to the idea and where people are interested in trying to take from others. It's just a smash-and-grab mentality. This mentality really endangers black and brown people.

Orelus: So what do you think public intellectuals should do in order to help coconstruct a socially just society?

Asante: Well, that's a good question. I hope you don't cast me as some public intellectual, because I'm not. I am an intellectual activist. That's how I call myself. I have no career motivations. I don't seek to be on television or in the press or anywhere. They may put me on television or the press, but that's not what I'm seeking. I have to play the role of being the best human that I can be, the most honest human that I can be, and the most reasonable human being that I can be.

I'm a rationalist. I cannot stand irrationality, and I can't stand pomposity. I can't stand pompous nonsense. I speak in unity with the oppressed because their condition calls for the utmost response to their situation. For me Afrocentricity itself is a massive opposition to the serious racial and cognitive aggression about the nature of the universe. Who named the stars before the Europeans? Who called the days of the week? Who made the calendar? Who crossed the seas before the Europeans did? Who articulated the concept of the divine? Who even gave the name to the gods? These were African people. Ana Monteiro-Ferreira has written in her book, *The Demise of the Inhuman*, that African cultural values might afford us the opportunity to interrogate new ways of being in the world.

My role in helping to construct a just society is always to uncover and smash ignorance wherever I see it. That's my role. I see that role as one that you can play even outside the press. I do it with my students and with my family. I teach. That is what I do. I take teaching seriously as a sacred task; to teach is to be a part of a vast priesthood entrusted to mediate between the sages and the young.

Orelus: I appreciate your work. As you are speaking, you remind me of Brother Walter Rodney.

Asante: Walter Rodney had an important influence on me. When he was killed, I happened to be in Nigeria. I had seen him earlier that year. He had a profound impact on me. Walter Rodney is one of my heroes. There's no question about it. I have many heroes, because the African world has produced enormous heroes. That's another discussion that you will have to record. The whole structure of the American society was designed essentially out of slavery and racism and consequently, like the struggle in South America, the one right here in our country has given us brilliant and courageous fighters for justice.

Orelus: So what has led you to focus your research and activism on Afrocentricity? And what has sustained you throughout those years in the struggle?

Asante: What happened to me was something very simple. I happened to live in Buffalo, New York, in the late 1970s. The condition of black people in Buffalo, New York, in the 1970s was the same as the conditions of black people today. We argued about the same problems and we debated the various strategies for conquest, but the critical solution had been suggested by Maulana Karenga in his critique of culture many years earlier. The central crisis in the black community, he had argued, was cultural. This was not merely a song-and-dance idea, but rather a substantive discourse on the nature of what constitutes values in the African American community.

I could not understand why this was so, that is, why the cultural crisis remained at the center of our social and economic condition. I had studied several movements, personalities, and legacies, much like many black intellectuals still do today, and I wrote *Afrocentricity* to express my concern about the state of my community. Later I would write *The Afrocentric Idea, An Afrocentric Manifesto*, and other books and articles as explanatory treatises on the central idea of agency. I discovered that our condition was one. We had never seen ourselves in the light of ourselves.

In other words, we've always seen ourselves as being secondary, not secondary to the Asians or to the Mexicans, but secondary to Europeans. It didn't make much sense to me then. Reading C. L. R. James, Cheikh Anta Diop, John Henrik Clarke, and others helped me understand a whole lot of what black people could achieve and have achieved. Such an understanding led me to concentrate on understanding first of all my own ground because I knew that I was a good student.

I went to the University of California in Los Angeles. I got my Ph.D. from the whites there, so I learned all about Western culture. But I didn't even know my own ground. It was only when I went deeper and deeper into my own ground that I became more intelligent. I became smarter. Years later when I met Cheikh Anta Diop in Dakar, Senegal, I had a basis for conversation with the greatest African intellectual of the era.

My early books were really written out of the whole idea of activism. I tried to write something that would be meaningful for the long term.

I've been sustained in the struggle by knowing that there are two texts written about African people. One text is the so-called mainstream white text and the other is the mainstream black text.

Now the mainstream white text writes about black people and makes them a footnote to the white struggle. The mainstream black text writes about black people as being centered in the struggle for justice. And that's the text I want to be in because I seek no personal glory or aggrandizement from those who neither appreciate nor accept the brilliance that exists in the African community.

I honestly don't care about the mainstream white text because I know I will be a footnote even with seventy-seven books. In the mainstream black text I work my way to the point that ultimately and hopefully, by living a ethical life, I will become an ancestor. That is my dream. In fact, that's my religion. My religion is to work my way to become an ancestor whose activism for *Maat* speaks for itself.

Orelus: If you have a piece of advice to give to younger scholars of color, what would that be?

Asante: The first one would be to advance on all fronts. You start from your intellectual ideas based on what you know fundamentally about your own historical experiences. You start there if you're going to be in philosophy and education. Did you grow up in Brooklyn? Where did you grow up?

Orelus: No. I grew up in Haiti.

Asante: Well, you have the best laboratory. Imagine if I had grown up in Haiti, what I would have been? I would have been powerful. I walked where Dessalines walked. I embraced Toussaint L'Ouverture and saw him betrayed, and I went up to La Citadelle La Ferièrre, and I meditated with the ancestors at Bois Caïman and breathed the air of Boukman. Who can touch that?

NINE

Taking a Stance for Equity and Fairness

Maxine Greene Speaks

Orelus: Could you please tell me how you think social justice has informed your work?

Greene: I hope it has. I hope I've talked about a fair distribution of opportunity and the use of social imagination for distribution of possibilities.

Orelus: Can you say more about this?

Greene: Which one? About social justice?

Orelus: Yes, social justice.

Greene: What do I think it means?

Orelus: Yes.

Greene: I think it means a fair distribution of opportunity. Social justice must be a ground for the distribution of possibilities.

Orelus: For more than half of a century, you have written extensively about a wide range of issues, such as equity, social imagination, and freedom.

Greene: Yes.

Orelus: You have also written about gender issues.

Greene: Gender, yes.

Orelus: So how do you see gender, equity, and social imagination are connected to social justice?

Greene: Social imagination is related to the concept of possibility of what might be, and it's hard to think about justice except imaginatively projecting possibility. Social justice informs my work. I hope when I've talked about education, for example, I haven't forgotten about the need to work for an equal distribution of opportunities, and support for young people in such a way that they don't have to suffer from inequalities. We have to support the development of literacy that is attuned to justice. The achievement gap between poor and affluent students has to be part of the equation.

Orelus: What do you think needs to be done to bridge that gap?

Greene: What should be done?

Orelus: Yes.

Greene: I suppose we need to change the system but in the meantime we have to understand the social and the economic reasons for that achievement gap. The achievement gap is not due to a gap in ability between poor and affluent students. The gap is due to a lack of support and a lack of understanding to what education ought to be. I think it's very important to realize what we see as a gap is not necessarily a gap in ability, a gap in understanding. It's a gap due to lack of support and marginality. It's a gap inflicted upon all range of children and grown-ups. But it's not due to an inherent inability. Is that clear?

Orelus: Yes, it is. Do you think that factors such as race, gender, and class have something to do with the achievement gap?

Greene: Yes. I certainly do. Certain people are pushed to the margins; they are excluded and forced into what some people call a culture of silence. The achievement gap should not be understood as a kind of inability on the part of some people. Achievement gap is not due to the fact that some people are dumb and some people are smart. It's primarily due to a lack of opportunity and support. We've never tried to distribute opportunity the way we should except for the privileged few.

Orelus: To what extent does gender play a role in widening the gap between girls and boys?

Greene: I think it's real in many institutions. There is a kind of forced marginality on girl students, and it's part of the general inequality that has characterized our society. But there has been much change because of the feminist movement and insistence on a real equality among different boys and girls. As we know, for a long time women and girls were definitely considered inferior people. I think it's less likely now because we've named gender inequality.

Orelus: What do you think of Obama's Race to the Top policy?

Greene: I object to the whole notion because I think a race to the top inevitably leaves some people at the bottom. There wouldn't be a top if there were no bottom. To me, the idea of a race perpetuates the inequality we're fighting because you don't have a race. You have unequal people running after each other. I don't know if that makes sense.

Orelus: It makes perfect sense. Would you like to say more about Obama's Race to the Top educational policy?

Greene: Yeah. It bothers me. It comes down to the equal distribution of opportunity. Race to the Top can mean anything, but subjugation of some people means they can't run as fast as others.

Orelus: In your opinion, what do we need to do to live in a socially just society?

Greene: What should we do? We have to change the system in order to live in a socially just society. You cannot allow income inequality; you can't allow that narrow space between the 99 percent and the 1 percent. If we ignore the economic aspect as well as the philosophic aspect of this issue, we can't move any further.

Orelus: Speaking of the 1 percent versus 99 percent, I am curious to know what you think of what's been happening with the Occupy movement.

Greene: I don't think it's extended far enough. I don't think people understand what it means. I don't think enough representatives in the population are included. I certainly support the Occupy movement because it has something to do with equity and justice and not taking over. This important part ought to be considered. I don't know if that's what you're asking?

Orelus: Yes, it is. Now I wish to engage you in the exploration of a philosophical question linked to social justice issues, particularly connected to teaching and learning. From your standpoint, what does it mean to teach for social justice?

Greene: First of all, it means to make students aware of what it means to live in an unjust society. They just have to look around and ask themselves if they are looking down on some people. Are they giving extra support to the ones who start with lack of opportunities? I think we need to stir young people to be outraged when they confront inequities in our society.

Orelus: So what do you think teachers should do in order to help build a society that is just?

Greene: Oh my god! Part of it has to do with literacy, a kind of social literacy. Also, part of it has to do with encouragement of exceptional imagination, somehow having a vision of what an equitable society ought to be like. Achieving this takes imagination; it takes economic understanding, and it takes many human capacities for the kind of opportunity we hope for.

Orelus: You have written and published extensively about many issues, and you've been doing this for more than half of a century. So what kind of influence do you think your work might have had on students, teachers, and public intellectuals?

Greene: It's very hard, and I can't claim any success. I can only claim opening a few doors that might be what capacity we have to encourage in order to achieve what is now a vision. What is now something we just ought to achieve?

Orelus: Going back to Obama's Race to the Top school policy, I wonder if you have any additional thought.

Greene: The whole idea of the difference between the bottom and the top bothers me. I object to the metaphor of the race—I object to the idea of the race, and I object to the idea of a society divided between a bottom and a top. I think we ought to change the metaphor. I think we ought to see how people with a whole variety of capacities should be encouraged but not one that dominates. There ought to be a range of possibilities, a range of imaginative visions. Not all the same. Really pursuing a diversity allowing for differences among young people and older people. That's the best I can do now.

Orelus: If you had to give advice to teachers and students, what would that be?

Greene: I would ask teachers to go beyond a professional or an institutional status position. I would ask that students refuse to submit to fixed authority, to question each other, and to question the people who claim to be the dominators in this society.

Orelus: What would you like to be remembered for?

Greene: I can only see myself making a small difference in opening the doors. I hope that people will have a vision of doors opening if they push fast enough and with enough imagination.

Orelus: Can you share with me a little bit about your background? You have been doing this for sixty years or more. Tell me a little bit about your journey.

Greene: I don't take a very optimistic view. But I still made myself, as old as I am, to awaken as many people as I can. And I put great emphasis upon imagination, on possibility, on resistance, and on the ability to be angry when things are unjust. What I feel I took for granted were the privileges I had. As time went by—partly through art, partly through paying attention, and partly through education—I began to notice injustices, and I tried to do whatever I could to compensate for the injustices that have fed my own privilege.

TEN

Anticolonial Thought and Indigenous Ways of Knowing and Doing

George Sefa Dei Speaks

Orelus: Let me begin by saying that the main focus of the book is social justice. How has social justice, broadly defined, informed your work?

Dei: I asked for guidance from the ancestors, Elders, and the Creator in sharing my thoughts with you. I know I speak here building on the wisdom, ideas, and thoughts of predecessors, colleagues, students, parents, and community workers I have encountered over the years. These individuals as a collective have shared knowledge with me. I can only reciprocate such knowledge by acknowledging that my ideas are not just my own thoughts but building on our collective wisdom, knowledge, and learning.

I will ask that you present my thoughts as you hear them, that is, in my own way of speaking and not restricted by the consumption required by the academic requirements that continually ask us to speak "intelligibly." I also want to sound a caution on my entry point into this dialogue as a Black body. I speak with a distinctively Black voice. It is not the only voice, but I definitely make no apologies for using this particular voice however contested. This is my own way of speaking and knowing how to speak.

I'm glad you've talked about defining social justice not just broadly, but also, recognizing that there are different dimensions of social justice, and that, for example, treating everybody the same is not the only model of social justice. There needs to be a recognition of the historic injustices that we, as oppressed and colonized peoples, have dealt with. We have to move away from the liberal notion that one talks about one form of social justice.

In effect, social justice for all, that's the ideal. I think we need to work towards that ideal. But given the inequities that already exist—if this is the right phrasing—we need to talk about other models of social justice. I think when you end up with a brand new social justice for all, you continue to reproduce the inequities that exist. Sure, the ideal of social justice is where we should be moving to. But we are not there yet.

We have to recognize history and also begin to talk about relative complexities while accepting our collective responsibilities in the fight for social justice. But we must also speak about social justice in the context of impositional and dominating ideas and practices, and the urgency for countervisioning social justice through other prisms such as Indigenous ways of knowing. We must affirm and hold to the idea of "something different is possible" if we are going to be true to ourselves in speaking about social justice for all. We can begin to have such conversation if we accept the possibilities of Indigenous and anticolonial conceptions of social justice.

Orelus: Let me ask you another question that's related to the first one. For decades you have written prolifically about a wide range of oppression, including racism, colonialism, and white supremacy. So how would you link these forms of oppression to social justice issues?

Dei: First of all, I think oppressions are connected: that is racism and the whole idea of white supremacy. We can't leave out colonialism because it was and still is very racist, patriarchal, and homophobic. So we need to look at racism and colonialism at the same time. We need to recognize that the colonized was a racially subjugated group and that the racially dominant group was white.

We have to go back to the history of colonialism to understand that. So you see the connection: what the white identities signify, what whiteness as a system also signifies. These are the products of colonialism that have been created in many ways to help reproduce racism, sexism, and homophobia which is based on this ideal of one group or one identity is better than the other, right? You see the connection there.

But just as racism and colonialism are connected, so is racism and other forms of oppression like sexism, patriarchy, classism, homophobia, ableism, heteronormativity, et cetera. These oppressions, as many scholars have taught us, are all connected. We cannot speak about one and not the other. But I am sure others more grounded will speak about these interconnections in this volume.

This wider discussion is also connected to the whole idea of social justice. Social justice calls for understanding under confluences, in fact two confluences to be exact: First, the recognition of *the presence of power, domination, and privilege.* Hence, the fight for social justice should be about power and privilege. How do we share power among ourselves, right? In that contest how do you share power among different groups? So, one is the recognition of the fight for social justice has to be about *power*.

Second, it also has to address *the sense of entitlement* that some people have. A powerful minority feel they are entitled to certain things without ever being able to understand how that has come about in terms of history and the so-called process. So that sense of entitlement can't go on without responsibility to history and the fact that important contemporary fundamental issues need to be addressed. But there's also the issue about how certain things became the tacit normal. Something about this: the late Joe Kincheloe and Shirley Steinberg talk about whiteness as a tacit norm that everyone references.

To me, the question of knowledge, knowledge production is critical to decolonization. We need to understand what it means to talk about whiteness, a system of dominance and oppression. While whiteness has many limitations, I also want to talk about it in terms of possibilities. What does it mean in terms of what we do with it? For example, one using their white identity to open doors for social justice work? I think we need to do more.

If you're going to stick with your privilege and only use it to produce more privilege for one, it becomes a problem. To me, one of the ways to look at it is that the fight for social justice has to be able to link issues of racism, colonialism, and white supremacy, and questions of complicities, responsibilities, and accountability. Racism is still ongoing, and colonialism has not ended. And we live white supremacy every day if we want to look at it in terms of systemic oppressions that we find ourselves in. We also need to talk about the possibility and the way social justice works. That allows us to address some of these problems and challenges.

But there is also something I want to add. Colonialism is about the land, and the question of race and Indigeneity has been on my mind for some time now. Being a participant on settled lands implicates us in the question of white colonial settlerhood. We must thus be able to define our collective responsibilities to the land and the peoples who have graciously allowed us to be on their lands. Of late I have vigorously spoken against this presence on Indigenous lands as occupation, which is about settlerhood. I disagree with any assertion that black bodies on this land are settlers given that settlerhood is about genocide, land dispossession and violence. For me, as an African Indigene it must allow us to articulate our responsibilities and implications to the Indigenous peoples on whose land we choose or are forced to stay.

Orelus: In many of your talks I looked up on YouTube focusing on racial issues, you have brilliantly pointed out how certain racial and ethnic groups, particularly blacks, have been marginalized. So in concrete terms, what would you propose be done to challenge the way they have been misrepresented and mistreated in society?

Dei: First we need to say this without fear and reprisals. We cannot be silenced over our marginality. And yes, these days we hear about Black lives and how our lives are deemed not worthy. By this I mean Black lives have always been deemed dispensable and disposable. We are disposable goods. We need to fight this scourge on intellectual thinking. Our lives matter and cannot be wasted the way, for example, we see police brutality manifest itself all across North America and Europe. We need to fight the idea where segments of our communities think they can dispense with Black lives with much impunity.

Many in society would deny and never acknowledge the fact that we have the disposability of Black lives. This lack of acknowledgment and recognition is a big struggle for all colonized, racialized, and Indigenous peoples. I think the sacrifice is on the acknowledgments. We need to acknowledge the problem; there's a lot of denial. The question you just asked me, you know what, there are some people around who would say that that's not true, that Blacks are not misrepresented and mistreated.

We need to acknowledge the historic injustices, the mistreatments, the devaluations, the negations, and the omissions. Acknowledgment is very important. And then we need to move beyond it and take concrete action addressing some of the inequities and injustices. Addressing these problems has to be our target as educators. To me, I see education as raising consciousness about the problem and also a willingness and commitment to do something to address it. That's very important.

I have always believed the marginalized cannot and should not hold up their arms and hope that somebody will bring to them manna from heaven. We have to empower ourselves and be able to do certain things for ourselves. We cannot continue to talk about the "European-ization of our minds." We have to recognize the power of our minds; we have to recognize our faults and practices. We need to think through solutions to the problems that affect our communities. Solidarities are welcome, but we should design our own futures. We should do so through critical education and anticolonial education, one that makes one aware of one's responsibilities, their collective responsibilities, and their place in history. We have to resist oppression; this is part of the puzzle to our lived experiences. Education is very important for community building. It's also going to empower ourselves in that process; education is very important.

Orelus: Like in the United States, the resource gap between dominant and subjugated groups in Canada is getting wider every year, if not every day. What do you think needs to be done to bridge such a gap?

Dei: The gap is widening as we speak. To me, part of the problem is that we have corporate capital greed, which needs to be critically looked at. We need to look at the consequences of certain things. Our inaction is always a drawback to forward movement. To what extent is the responsibility being shared creating jobs for wealth and prosperity? There must be sharing responsibility.

To me, it's very important that we look at it in terms of power sharing. We have to look at also how some of our economic relations continue to widen the gap between the haves and the have-nots. We need to address that. We also need to recognize the community that we are a part of. It calls for sharing; it calls for mental reciprocity. We cannot simply talk about the power of the corporate capital or the power of capitalism.

We also have to be able to talk very concretely and honestly about some of the ills, the downfalls, and, in some cases, the disaster of our economic systems, as well as the disparity between those haves and have-nots. We must be able to have that conversation. We must be able to have that conversation because we cannot continue to live in a society where there is this widening economic and social gap between the haves and the have-nots. It's not healthy for a society, and so we need to address that. That's one way to address the gap. I think we all contribute to the problem when we are caught in a "creeping survivalism."

Orelus: Speaking of gap, what is your position on the Canadian school system? How has it treated students and professors of African descent and other minority groups?

Dei: Let me put it this way. It is still a "work in progress," meaning the job is not yet done. Listen, I don't want to sweep everything with a broom. I know that there are some committed educators around here in Canada. I also know people who are resistant to speaking on these issues. They would cry wolf whenever you say schools are failing our youth. And I think we need to recognize that. We also need to recognize there are risk takers around with good intentions.

Let me also add that sometimes good intentions are not the point. Intentionality is not enough. We have to find honest and courageous people to speak about the racial, educational, and socioeconomic disenfranchisement. So we need to hold accountable those in power for some of the problems we have to deal with. We have a long way to go to address all this we are speaking about. It needs a concrete commitment.

Part of the problem is the lack of honesty in admitting that we have a problem. How can you solve a problem when it is denied? So let us be intellectually and politically honest and admit that schools are not serving the needs of all our students. Schools have not been designed for all. Schools are for the most powerful, in terms of their values, ideologies, and intended consequences of schooling. It may as well be that we need to revisit schooling in its entirety.

We need to talk about how we create communities and communities of schooling where proposed knowledge is valued and where people's identities are respected. This is a question of power sharing. We can't just talk about history and not our responsibility to history. We need to address structural inequities, and the curriculum becomes a very important point in this undertaking.

How do we ensure that the curriculum addresses the needs, the concept, the aspirations, and the hopes of the diverse learners that we have in the school system today? How do we ensure that educators are committed to their students? How do we ensure that we support educators and provide education that is anticolonial, that is education that allows the learner to be empowered enough to ask critical questions, the questions that sometimes we want to put under the carpet that we don't want to embrace?

We also want to talk about education that holds us accountable to our communities because they are the communities that sustain us. If we have an education system that does not meet the need of our communities, what sort of education is that? We need to ask these questions. My point here is that the school system has a long way to go. There are questions about the curriculum, there are questions about instruction, there are questions about texts, there are questions about students' identities, and there are questions about knowledge production and value systems that need to be asked and addressed. There's so much liberal talk about schooling and education. I have always made the point that we have to be very careful, because we can sound very seductive and moral when we speak about these issues.

How do we hope to accomplish change by adding to what already exists? This question is relevant because, as I have continually argued, what already exists is the source of the problem in the first place. We need to step back and begin anew. We also need to have contact spaces outside the school system that allow us to address some of these issues. We've been speaking about those issues for far too long. They all pass us by, and there seems to be no change. So we need to look at the other options, counter visions of schooling which may be outside the dominant realm, and we need to think outside the box. And so that's my call.

We continue to talk about this and how it's imperative for the school system to meet the challenges of educating learners informed by the complexity of ideas and events that will shape growth and development. We need to ask questions about the school system, what it means to create an inclusive antiracist global future. What is the responsibility of the schools in creating that future? What is the role of anticolonial education? How do we decolonize the spaces of education so that the learners can feel a sense of self and collective worth and pride, a sense that their knowledge counts, that they bring a body of knowledge and that knowledge is relevant. How do we frame education to make learners human again, talking about importance of history, identity, and culture in a very critical way? How are we connected as communities of learners?

Orelus: Based on your professional and personal experiences and observation as a researcher and an educator, what are some of the challenges that teachers and professors of color have been facing in both the Canadian and U.S. school systems?

Dei: Acknowledgment, recognition, and validation of our knowledges, experiences, histories, and identities rather than devaluations and insignificance. And I am speaking about such recognition on the dominant's terms. On our own terms, however contested. We talk about the challenges of how we can make schools very inclusive, right? Do we validate multiple knowledges that our learners have and bring to school? How do we create a space that allows the educator to be able to actualize the hopes and dreams of the learners? How do we address questions of racism, sexism, and homophobia? How do we address questions of structural inequities?

It's a call for collective response to that. It's very important we do not sit in the ivory tower. We have to be grounded in communities. We have to be grounded in communities. Our work has to be able to combine intellectual scholarship and community politics. We have to be able to find a way to talk about the dependence of scholarship and will and political desire to bring about change, transformation. We have to address that.

We have a system in place where educators combine scholarship with community work and activism because education at the end of the day has to produce change; it has to produce effect. It has to make concrete change in the lives of our learners, in the lives of our communities—and that's the challenge we have to take on. We need to develop what I would call an anticolonial decolonial intellectuality that allows us to combine our intellectual scholarship with political work and courage that makes a difference.

Orelus: So in your opinion, George, what does it mean to live in a socially, racially, and economically just society?

Dei: The envisaged society will be a messy, welcoming utopia. But it can be real and actualized. It seems the question itself is self-actualization. And that's very important. I think when one is able to actualize their hopes and dreams. When one doesn't have to worry about somebody thinking they are less than capable, less than human, and less than intellectual than him or her because of that person's racial, gender, class, or sexual background. There's a need to recognize our relative contributions to existing stereotypes.

Also, when we have a sense that we are a community, a community that shares ideas, identities, and experiences. That's the society we need to build. I will call it a messy utopia. Going from the notion of utopia, I have called it a "messy utopia." It's going to be contested; it's not going to be fine and dandy. We are going to ruffle feathers. We are going to get on the nerves of those who want to keep the system the way it is. We need to put on the table questions of colonialism, imperialism, race, class, [dis]ability, sexuality, and gender; questions about our responsibilities to the land on which we settle or in which we find ourselves.

To me, a socially, racially, and economically just society is a society that's fulfilling our dreams, hopes, and aspirations. I think it's very important to talk about those issues. It's important to talk about this as something that can only be accomplished. We need to recognize questions of power. I don't want this blind liberal talk about allyship. It is not because we are in this together we don't have to deal with power issues, we don't have to deal with structural inequities, and that only talking about it somehow will solve the problem. We have to deal with these issues. To me, that's very important of solidarity.

Orelus: From your standpoint, what role do you think activist public intellectuals should play in coconstructing such a society?

Dei: We have to be activist scholars. We also have to be world academic warriors. We have to be fighters. These are all decolonized undertakings that actually bring about difference, and that difference is very important. I think we also need to talk about power sharing. You can't have a racially just society when you don't address the question of power sharing.

We also have to look at the communities that have been disenfranchised along the lines of race. We need to be able to put that on the table. We have to have an honest discussion about race. It is not just about blackness or not just about the Indigenous body. Race is also about white. What does that mean when you talk about race that's white? It comes back to the question that you asked me before: How do we deal with questions on the normalization of whiteness? How sometimes whiteness must recess as neutral, objective, innocent, and as desirable?

To me, public intellectuals have a role to play there; we have to talk about complicities. I think many of us are complicit. We don't want to ruffle feathers that are so comfortable and cocooned. Many of us don't want to speak out because they know if they do they might pay a price. Sometimes we have to be able to recognize when our fears prevent us from speaking. By not speaking out against racism, sexism, homophobia, you contribute to racism, sexism, and homophobia. You cannot be neutral. There's nothing like the place of neutrality in the presence of injustice and inequity.

How do we address questions of complicities and responsibilities in that undertaking? We also have to deal with this sense of entitlement. We cannot have this sense of entitlement. It's so problematic when it's not much with any discussion of responsibility and accountability. This is very important in that undertaking. Public intellectuals have a role to play in building this society because they're people who will listen to us, right? What good is what we say if what we say does not make a difference? I always make this point. At the end of the day, we have to recognize that we have to collectively make it happen.

Orelus: How about power relationships among unequal groups in society affecting the lives of many? What do you say about these relationships?

Dei: Yes, sometimes this is the nature of colonial oppression. The oppressed group turns their oppression inwards and begins to oppress others. There are many examples in history and in contemporary society to go by. When we talk about power, we have to talk about it in terms of discretionary use of power. How do we use our power to address questions of injustice and inequities? How do we use our opposition to further the cause of information? How do we use our role as intellectuals to ask critical questions?

Orelus: A related question: There's been a great deal of studies done on race, racism, and whiteness. To what extent do you think these studies have contributed to improve the human conditions of the less fortunate black and brown people?

Dei: First of all, as you and I know, not everything called race studies is about race studies. In fact some studies purported to be about oppressed groups end up oppressing us further. We become victims, hapless, and lack agency. Nonetheless, critical race and antiracism studies would bring to the fore questions of power and privilege, which is very important. There are also studies that actually reproduce the status quo.

We need to talk about antiracist politics and structures contributing to our present condition of existence. How are the structures contributing to the inequities that we are faced with? I think putting those questions on the table is very important. As I said, we need to begin to talk about the questions of responsibilities and complicities and their implications. I would make a distinction between critical studies that put on the table questions of domination, power, and privilege and those studies that help reproduce the status quo.

Orelus: You are highly respected in many academic and intellectual circles in Canada and beyond. Have you ever had to battle institutional racism despite of your fame? If so, how have you strategically dealt with it?

Dei: It is not easy to speak about race in the academy. I have observed that as a racial minority scholar one can go "far" in the academy by being silent on race. You can even put your own people under the bus and be deemed very intellectual and scholarly. What kind of scholarship is that? Make someone feel good? All the same we cannot afford not to ask questions about race and racism just as we talk about gender, sex, and homophobia. That's very important for anybody whose life has to contend with that. Because we speak about these issues, we are seen as anti-intellectuals.

We are seen as troublemakers creating problems when one doesn't exist. That's just a problem we have to deal with. When you speak with a different accent, there are people who think you are less than them. If you are facing these issues that people don't want to hear about, they accuse you of creating, fermenting trouble when and where it doesn't exist. We also have to talk about the school system and be mindful of the curriculum in terms of diversity issues. These issues are real. The whole question of validation of knowledge is important. Some kinds of knowledge are validated while others are not. Those are issues that many people are confronted with daily.

At the end of the day, what you have is a contest of knowledge. We are contesting the future, right? It cannot be just about knowledge; it is grounded in politics, in community politics. The affirmation of communities is very important and good for spiritual healing. We are dismembered; we have dismembered souls. So we need that healing. We take the healing process from the notion of community; it is grounded in the community from which we get support. That's what I mean by saying every rationalized intellectual has to be involved in his or her community.

I am not going to scribe community politics, but one must be able to speak to community politics, which is different from scribing. We create communities. So, to me, being able to define the community and working within sustains individuals and helps them heal and regenerate their strength and soul.

I am deeply spiritual. I don't know whether you know or not. I'm a traditional elder, a chief in Ghana. You cannot be a chief without being spiritual. We believe in the power of ancestors—somebody who continues to watch over us, guide us, and protect us. There is a relationship with the Creator; the divine; and the mother earth. This is very important. It sustains the way we do our work. Those are the things that help to sustain me in terms of the work that I do.

I also want to mention that the sort of support I get comes from many of the graduate students I work with. So communities and students are very important in my own work. Being able to mentor students who grow up to become professors is very important, because at the end of the day these are the students that respect you, as they know that you will give them something different. They also have a responsibility to give back. We need to talk about giving back to our communities. So those are my answers.

A long time ago I raised the question of whether we are prepared to assume the responsibility of building communities. Being able to build a community with your students and outside the academy is very important because these are the sense of connections that we need to become individuals connected to communities. That's how we build our strength and our responsibility.

Orelus: You have written many books on Frantz Fanon. How has his anticolonial work on race and racism influenced yours?

Dei: Everyone knows Frantz Fanon is an anticolonist theorist. But he was also a practitioner. I mean, he was somebody who was in the trenches; he was with guerrilla warfare. That's very important. I think he speaks from experience. He noted the psychic and psycho-existential reality of blackness, race, and the colonized body. His theorizing from experience has influenced me, as well as his ideas about balance. How have we come to understand balance? We have to understand balance in its complex and varied forms.

We have to understand balance of the colonial and balance of colonialism. We have to understand our responsibilities in resisting that balance. And what it means to talk about creating one's humanity. I'm influenced by those ideas. I'm also influenced by his ideas on blackness. We have to look at blackness in a way that equates blackness with balance, with community, and we have to be able to work with that humanity. I'm also very influenced by his ideas of the sinful new humanity.

This new humanity is going to be something that requires that we do not fold up our arms. We have to struggle. We have to fight for a new humanity. Fanon talks about the need to challenge our colonial investments and privileges. It seems we are invested in our own coloniality much more than in our anticoloniality. We need to resist that; we need to challenge that. You cannot create an antiracist, anticolonial global future, and a new humanity without resistance. The product of colonialism and colonialization has not ended, so the political decolonizing cannot end.

To me, these are powerful ideas one has to work with. When we speak of a society of racism and a society of oppression, I think it's very important to understand it in terms of what risks it has in mind. When he talks about equalizing the mind, I think he picks up on this notion. He talks about racist colonization, which makes you feel that you are inferior; it leaves you with this complex to the point where sometimes you feel that you always have to react. You have to change that, because we don't always have to react. We can design our own future. True struggle is being able to resist and create one's humanity. To me, this is very important.

Orelus: Allow me to formulate another question related to the previous one. In one of your books, you have made an interesting statement about Steve Biko's book, I Write What I Like, *which you claim to be your favorite book. I am curious to know in what way and to what degree Biko has influenced you?*

Dei: I don't claim I mean it. That is the dominant thought. I mean what I say. I appreciate Steve Biko's honesty. His notion about black consciousness is very powerful. Why should we be concerned about a problem that we didn't create? Biko asked. We have to have an answer for that. We have to be concerned because, as I said before, colonialism hasn't ended. These are different ways colonialism plays itself out. It plays itself out through imposition of race, class, and gender through socialization.

We have to address the notion about "I write what I like." To me, we have to write from our hearts. Of course, we write for an audience, but it must come from our hearts. If you don't believe what you are saying, don't write it. Anybody who writes simply for the sake of scholarship is a general intellectual. I think we have to believe in what and why we write.

Fighting for social justice and against inequities has to come from the heart. We are searching for a better world where we respect and validate one another, share resources, and deal with power—a world where all can relate, not in the sense that everything goes but with the sense that recognizes that everybody has a contribution to make, that everybody matters, that everybody counts.

We cannot live in a world where people have this sense of hopelessness, a sense of living a dead-end existence, a sense of stolen dreams. It's not going to be a healthy world for communities at large. I think we have to talk about that sense of community, and how we create that. To me, that must come from the heart. It has to come from the heart if we are to honestly believe in it.

Orelus: As you know, no one has ever made it on his or her own. Along the way, someone has helped and inspired us. Trace for me, a little bit, your professional trajectory. Who has helped you along the way?

Dei: I'm glad you're asking this as one of your final questions, because it's very appropriate to end with that question. No matter what you have achieved, someone has helped you along the way. A lot of people have helped me. I need to talk about my mother. When my dad died, she was the one who brought us up. She made a lot of sacrifice to take care of us, me and my sibling.

Let me talk about the place where I grew up, the friends that I made and how they were very helpful. We were there for each other. We got each other's back covered. I think we also have to talk about how and when we come to the academy, the committees we are part of, and, of course, the students. Sometimes you meet colleagues who have been very helpful. You share some ideas with them and they are very supportive of your work. A collective of people have helped me along the way. My only hope is that I do not disappoint this collective us. There is an African saying, "I am because we are, and because we are therefore I am."

Orelus: Who has been your most influential role model?

Dei: There's no bigger role model to me than my mother. Currently, she suffers from dementia. She is not speaking much at all. One of the things I always hope that I will never do is to disappoint her because of the sacrifice she made for us. There are many people whom I have encountered, who have helped and influenced me. I've been influenced by many scholars. Many community politics have also been very influential and at the same token contain certain limitations. Sometimes you wonder why you have been able to uphold the ideas, thoughts, and practices that these people actually had in mind. This is always a work in process. We are always building on ourselves and communities. We have to recognize our limitations. Otherwise, we will not succeed.

ELEVEN

The Politics of Representation

A Social Justice Issue

Stuart Hall Speaks

Orelus: Social justice has been at the center of many educational and political debates. How has this concept informed your work?

Hall: I'll just say that in all honesty, it's not a concept that I personally have used a lot. This is very important to me as a kind of background. It's one of the wider purposes of my intellectual life, as well as my political life. Social justice has a very specific content, and I have not written about that content in that form.

So what I'm saying is that it has informed my work in so far as I work in cultural studies, or in race, or in representation; all has a long-term intention of contributing to greater social justice in the world. Social justice as such is itself a more specific term, which has come into use more recently. And I don't know whether you want to pursue that or not, but perhaps not. I mean that you won't find social justice written throughout my work.

Orelus: I'm aware of that. In your work you have talked about representation, cultural and racial issues, and Marxism. I was just curious to know to what extent you think these issues you have explored through your scholarly and political work are connected to social justice.

Hall: Well, they are all connected in different ways. Let's start with representation: how you represent groups, whether you stereotype

119

them, whether you acknowledge their role in history, whether you appreciate the differences between different members of the same group, whether you don't judge them according to some general standard, whether they're more civilized than others, or more barbaric than others, representation does affect how we think about, see, and imagine other people. Of course, that's the question of social justice.

Cultural and racial issues have a very broad feel in culture depending on what you mean by it. Let's take the narrow definition of culture, as an example. In cultural practices, they're related to social justice in a number of ways. Culture is about the language of how things are represented, thought about, et cetera. But if you talk about culture as an area of production and work, as a question of access, that is, who has access to cultural expression? Or does everybody have something like equal access? The answer is no.

That means that culture is contrary to what a lot of people think it is— it is power. Some people have more power in culture and cultural representations than others. Power is tremendous, persistent, and systematic. The question of social injustice, I think, speaks for itself. It's an example of all the things I've just said.

If you divide populations along racial difference and then one sector of a population regards another sector of the population as less worthy, less intelligent, driven more by emotion than by reason, not capable of advanced thought and thinking, not sophisticated, not complex, these are forms of inequality because multiple forms of consequences follow from that. That affects what they earn, what position they hold in society, the respect in which they are regarded in society. Different racial groups have different health rates, death rates, and illness. So it affects the entire life experiences, life chances, possibilities, and outlook of groups that are being unjustly treated. Those are some of the consequences—don't know whether you want to pursue that.

Orelus: Thank you so much for making the linkage between representation and social justice. In many of your talks focusing on representation, you have shown ways in which certain racial-ethnic groups, particularly minority groups, have been misrepresented in the media and society at large. Is it fair to argue there might be a certain agenda behind ways in which certain groups are represented in society?

Hall: Yes, I've written about those questions. I think they are very important, but I just want to enter a small reservation. I'm not terribly happy about the notion of misrepresentation because misrepresentation suggests intention. People go out to falsify or tell untruths about another group or represent them in ways that they know to be untrue. Let us acknowledge that a great deal of that goes on.

If you're trying to exert political or economic power over another group, one of the ways in which you do so is by representing who you are and what you are capable of doing. This is connected to distribution of life choices, resources, and so on. It's a very important question, but we shouldn't restrict ourselves to that. A lot of misrepresentation is not intentional. Nobody sits down, has an agenda, and says: go out and misrepresent the writers, or go out and misrepresent black people, go out and misrepresent gay people, and so on.

It's not quite like that. Misrepresentation is more a question of what the structures are. What is taken for granted? What is not taken for granted? And people repeat that without necessarily having an agenda. Half of the time, they don't know what they're misrepresenting, but they are misrepresenting and it has real effect. So you mustn't limit the question to misrepresentation.

The conscious intentions of a well-established agenda, which some groups have in relation to others, must be carefully analyzed. I'm not saying that doesn't exist, because it does exist and it's very important. But misrepresentation, as you call it, it is wider than that. Yes, it has to do with structures of apprehension, of how people see others. And those things are shaped by long-term historical purposes.

It sometimes happens without people being conscious of it. As Marx once said, it happens behind "men's and women's backs." And not consciously being pursued, but they're being pursued nonetheless and some people don't even know they are pursuing them. So that is a wider field than a misrepresentation agenda. Do you understand what I'm saying?

Orelus: Are you saying that groups that have been misrepresented are misrepresented out of ignorance? In other words, those who misrepresent "certain ethnic and racial groups" do so out of ignorance—they don't have any level of consciousness around this issue?

Hall: Well, sometimes. But I don't think it is ignorance. Look, let me try to give you an example. Suppose you live in a Western society where you've not encountered many black people. You've read about them, you've read the literature; you have read the newspaper, et cetera. You form the impression that black people do better in manual jobs than intellectual jobs, okay? Well, you are speaking to a student or speaking to a body of people, you might pass that on. You have to make a distinction in what individuals intend to do. What they're doing even when they don't intend it or are unconscious of it. There's unconscious misrepresentation.

Orelus: That makes sense. Of course, these factors matter whether they understand them or not. They have had real social, economic, political, educational, and political effects on the lives of misrepresented groups.

Hall: Yes. I suppose my answer is to your notion of an agenda. A notion of an agenda means that people meet around some imaginary table and consciously pursue certain purposes. They can pursue certain purposes not because they consciously mean it or even because they understand the status quo but because that's just how life is. The way of misrepresenting other people has become what I would call '"naturalized." It's partly nature. I don't think it's great or not great; it's how it is. And we must include that a certain level of unconscious misrepresentation of a conscious political agenda is being pursued.

Orelus: Well, it makes sense what you just articulated. I would like to proceed to ask you another question regarding cultural studies. You are considered one of the world leading cultural theorists.

Hall: I'm certainly not one of the world leading cultural theorists.

Orelus: I understand. In any case, in your humble opinion, to what degree have cultural studies as a discipline contributed to improving the conditions of the less fortunate, or to borrow Fanon's term, the wretched of the earth?

Hall: That is a very good question. I don't know that theory ever contributes directly to changing the social conditions of anybody. On the other hand, it's an essential element in understanding what is going on and informing how you should change it. So I wouldn't measure it by, well, "Have my theories gone out and have been picked up and people rioted as a result of it?" The connection isn't that simple.

But if what I've said over a long period of time had led certain individuals or groups to think about their situation in different terms, to examine the reasons why it is that way, to think about how we can change it, it has contributed, you might say, indirectly. I don't over-value cultural theory, but it has contributed indirectly to the actions of groups or individuals, including unfortunate people, who are still part of "the wretched of the earth." Cultural theory at its best supports their struggle. I want to give you two elaborations of that point.

When we were in the early days, that is, in the start of cultural studies at Birmingham University, where more contemporary cultures really began to come together, people used to say well, what is it for? Who does it help? I don't know if it directly helps anybody. It doesn't—it didn't make civil rights more effective. It didn't contribute directly to the struggle of South Africa. All these things were going on at the time. But those struggles were informed by the things that people were reading, thinking, and talking about. Cultural studies might have indirectly influenced and helped to guide, shape, and deepen their understanding. So understanding is the middle term, you understand me?

Cultural theory is necessary for understanding, and understanding is necessary for changing the world. Gramsci, an Italian Marxist theorist who I have learned a great deal from, has a slogan, "Pessimism of the intellect, optimism of the will." What that means is the function of intellectuals is not to tear everybody up, not necessarily to join the picket lines. That's not intellectual function. Intellectual function is telling the truth, as they really understand it to the best of their capacity.

Things are not going well now. Intellectuals have to say something, but they don't need to cheer up. I mean someone needs to say look: we've been in a better place than we are in the moment; we are in a pretty wretched place now. I think in some respects we are. Think about the impact of the economic recession on the lives of masses of people. It means we're in a poor situation. The same is true internationally. We, in Britain and the United States, are involved in a series of semi neocolonial wars—whatever it might be.

These days it's called humanitarian intervention. Whatever it's called, that's not good for any of the places that we're in. It's not my job to say: well, you did that but you were not right about it. My job is to say: You went into Afghanistan on certain grounds. You didn't understand the place. The consequences are you are fighting a war that you cannot win. So don't fool yourself in thinking that you are going to be successful there. I have made a contribution by saying what I think the situation is really like.

Some are a bit too hasty about cultural theory and intellectual work in general. They want ideas to have an immediate impact. They often don't have an immediate impact. They have a very profound indirect impact. And political action is nothing unless it is informed by a deep and profound understanding of what the real situation is. If the real situation is not very perspicuous to change, don't persuade people because it makes you feel good.

Orelus: Let's shift the conversation a bit. What is your assessment of the current U.S. president, Barack Obama?

Hall: I don't know what the state of play is in the coming election, of where it will be by the time the book is published, but I would say that Obama was a heroic, historic victory as the first black president of the United States. He really did not understand how powerful was the American political system that he was entering. He didn't understand how deeply it was rigged against change of any kind.

When you go out in the street and say: we're going to Washington and we're going to change it tomorrow, you fool yourself because you're not going to change it overnight. It requires many years of extreme, difficult struggles. And if you don't recognize that, or if some political theorist doesn't tell you that, you then run into trouble because you raise the expectation of your supporters and you can't deliver. You find yourself trapped rather than leading.

Orelus: Let me ask you a related question. Like in the United States, the resources gap between dominant and nondominant groups in the UK is getting wider every year. What do you think needs to be done to bridge such a gap?

Hall: Very crudely you can do only two things. One is to redistribute the resources better and more fairly between dominant and nondominant groups. Yes, you can reform the degree of inequality—not an easy thing to do because, to put it bluntly, you're living in a capitalist society. And capitalism depends on creating a gap between dominant and dominated and rich and poor. It depends on it.

They don't tell us that, but that is how it works. It makes some people very rich and other people extremely poor. So if you're going to change the political system or the economic system so that more resources go to the dominated and less to the dominant, you'll have a political fight on your hands. Now, another way is not just to redistribute the resources but to change the whole system with some other system.

Orelus: The problem about this approach is that we don't know what other system really would work and if it would be better than the one we have now.

Hall: I don't rule that out. Let me give you an example of distributing the resources better and fairly. The British welfare state or the New

Deal didn't change this whole system, but it did mean that some of the wealth and resources were redistributed to poor groups. It had a redistributionist philosophy. Who said rich people can afford to get good medical services when they're ill and poor people can't? In the UK what they did about that was to create the national welfare state; they also created a national health service.

Those are important, and to be honest, I would be extremely happy if more of them were around just at the moment. I think that's something we might really persuade people to support. What I'm not sure is on the table at the moment is getting rid of the whole capitalist system. The conditions are there for that radical degree of redistribution of wealth, assets, and property.

Orelus: So you're not convinced that we can dismantle the capitalist system?

Hall: Well, not today or after tomorrow. It doesn't mean that you can't. But it is not so simple dismantling capitalism. Do have any idea what you mean by that phrase, dismantle capitalism?

Orelus: That would require a profound transformation of the system and careful reconfiguration of power.

Hall: You mean revolution, in other words.

Orelus: That's correct.

Hall: You and I might want a world revolution, but this is not going to happen tomorrow.

The American population as well as the British population is not about to conduct a revolution or change the entire system. So when you asked me if I am not convinced about dismantling capitalism, I wanted to say that in the short term or medium term that it is not going to happen. It's my duty as an intellectual not to say: well, press on with it anyway. My duty as an intellectual is to say I don't think it's very likely. But I think we can do something better than what we are doing now. This includes raising the level of understanding so that people begin to see that it's not just the incidental distribution of resources that is wrong, it's the system itself,

One of the advances of the Occupy movement is that it has made clear that it's not just that some people are very rich and some people are very poor, but rather the economic system itself is systemic. If more people thought it was systemic, then you might be able to persuade a greater majority of people to say: well, then the problem is the system, not the greed of the capitalist or the rich. You had better change the system, and you will then get closer to—if not to a world revolution—to a very radical degree of social change, but we are not in that situation today. You look around the world and you can't put your hand on your heart and say that is the sense that you make of the world at the beginning of the twenty-first century. It's a pity, but that is how it is.

Orelus: Yes, indeed. In your opinion, what is it meant to be living in a socially just society?

Hall: I wouldn't know because I've never lived in one.

Orelus: But can we stretch our imagination to visualize or at least theorize how a socially just society might look in concrete terms?

Hall: A socially just society, which is more just than the one we have now, would be one in which the gap between the haves and the have-nots does not exist and where there would be a different feel to social life; that is, you would not judge people for who they are and because of their position in society. You would judge them as human beings. They deserve your respect even if they are not in a very eminent position in society. That would be very different from the one we have now—a society where everybody judges everybody else according to a hierarchy of what is success and what is not success. So those are two things, two aspects of how I imagine a socially just society, which is not just the case in the moment.

Socially just is just under a very broad category. What would that mean in the sphere of, say, sexuality? It would mean that there wouldn't be laws against same-sex relationships and that they wouldn't be marginalized. This would also mean they wouldn't be prevented from worshiping in church; they could make their commitment over life. So socially just then begins with being different as this applies to different areas of life.

Orelus: What role do you think public intellectuals and critical educators should play in building such a society?

Hall: Well, as I said, their duty is to understand the world better and to help other people politically understand how the system works, how it could be changed, and what are the risks and advantages of changing it in a certain way. That's what they can do—speak truth to power. That's how they help. That's not the only thing they can do. They're human beings, and they can go out and do some good in the world. As intellectuals, their intellectual function is not to be judged by whether they stand in front of some demonstration or not. It's to be judged by the contribution (or lack thereof) they have made to their own area of studies and an understanding of the world that might be conducive to social change.

Orelus: You are highly respected in the academic circle in the UK and beyond. Have you ever had to battle against institutional racism despite your fame? And if so, how have you done so?

Hall: I don't have a lot experience of actually working in institutions, which are deeply inflicted by racism. I worked in liberal universities. Do you understand me? They're not the areas where institutional racism affects me personally as much as it does in other areas. I'm not saying that it doesn't. It probably affected me very much.

My fame! I don't know about my fame. But certainly in the early days, I felt institutions were rigged against people like me. I went to work for the university and wasn't even sure if I should walk through the front door of the college; I didn't feel I belonged. So it's not that they tried to keep me out, but I was battling against an institutional culture, which was racially biased. But that is not really the important point. The important point is to understand how institutions work in society as a whole, whether they touch me personally or not. I've spent a lot of time trying to do that.

I took part in marches protesting the murder of a black boy. He was mugged and killed by five white boys at a bus stop in South London. His name was Stephen Lawrence. Bright kid who wanted to do architecture. On his way home peacefully, five men came up to him and, by the time they left, they stabbed him to death. There was a huge investigation into that incident, and why the police were unable or seemed unable to do very much about it, including unable to bring them to justice.

It's not only that some policemen are racist. It is that they live in a culture which institutionally operates according to racist practices. It doesn't advance black people as much as it advances whites. It doesn't pay women what it pays men. This is not a question of choice; do you understand me? It's a question of how the institution works. Whether the institution does it consciously or not is a debatable question.

It can be said that the British police is riddled with not just a few people with racist attitudes but with institutional racism. It is not that you have some bad apples in the police force or bad apples in the business world. The whole of this world is structured by racist beliefs whether one knows that or not. But gradually and slowly people will come to accept that institutional racism exists.

Institutional racism is not resolved by promoting one black person. It involves changing the system by which people are promoted generally. There is a difference between an individual and an institution or practice, and I hope some of my writing has contributed to the notion of institutional racism.

Orelus: So you have seen some progress?

Hall: Yes, of course, but it doesn't stop institutional racism. People are a bit more conscious about it. They've had to accept you, accept criteria for appointing people which specifically say you are not to attend to your gender, race, sexual identity, and so on. So those are important advances, not the whole victory, not the whole struggle, but they are important advances.

Orelus: Reflecting on your professional accomplishments and journey. What are some of the factors, you think, that might have contributed to your success?

Hall: I find this an almost impossible question to answer. I'm not being falsely modest. I don't think about my success. I feel my life incomplete; it's going somewhere; it continues to struggle for things. I do things, which later on, when I look back, I think that they were rubbish. So I wouldn't say it was a great success.

With regard to my professional accomplishments and journey, I really don't know. I mean I have the good fortune to be quite intelligent so I could benefit from the educational opportunities I got. Other people are just as intelligent, but they happen not to be in the same situation as me. I have made myself intelligent. So these are not things I think I've done which might have contributed to success, if success is what it is.

Orelus: You left Jamaica, your native land, when you were nineteen years old. During that era, Jamaica was still under British colony. So how has it been like to live in the UK coming from Jamaica as a colonized subject, if I may use that term?

Hall: Certainly, you may. I was a colonized subject. In fact, I was at the bottom of colonial pecking order. So yes, I was a colonized subject. I carried my British passport, which said that I was a subject of the British Empire and so on. That's how I came. Are you asking what was it like to leave Jamaica? Or what was it like to come here?

Orelus: Basically you have been sharing two worlds: Jamaica and the UK. So how do you understand the unequal colonial power relation between the colonized land, Jamaica, and the colonizing power, the UK?

Hall: In some ways, the answers are obvious. I had learned in my childhood and adolescence exactly what it meant to be a colonial, to be a colonized minority, to be a subordinate, and to be of lower social status. With all those things I had learned what colonization is. I was required to adapt who I was to the colonizing culture.

I spoke English. I went to an English-style public school. I learned French. I learned more history about Britain than I did about the Caribbean and so on. These are built-in structural distortions that colonialism imposes on young people. Growing up in that world, I was very unhappy about that, deeply unhappy. I was unhappy on two grounds. One is that I thought it was incredibly unjust exercise of economic political and cultural power—foreign group over other people. In the Caribbean not only did they exercise power over us, they actually took us from where we lived and punched us into slavery, in plantations society. This has created deep inequality in a very systematic way after three hundred years.

So why didn't I just stay in Jamaica? As a young person, you learn about other places. You know the ideas of working over there. You'd like to go to see what it's like. What makes them so powerful? What makes them so self-satisfied? What makes them think they are the lords of creation? Is it really so wonderful over there? So I was eager to go and see it. Actually there's a sort of paradox there because we were already in the era when direct colonialism was ending.

While national liberation and self-independence movements were taking place in Jamaica, I nevertheless wanted to encounter a bit of the rest of the world. I found it very hard since I was brought up in a rather conservative family, one in which members had too much respect for the colonial and the colonizing culture. I found being the son of a colored middle-class colonial family running against everything I believed. But it wasn't easy for me to find the way of acting differently in that world.

When I got to England, my sense of the colonizing country, colonizing culture, was a terrible place to live in, because immediately I arrived I encountered racism of a new, different, and more violent kind than I even encountered in the colonial world. There's a lot of racism in the colonial world, believe me. Why are you here? What are you doing here? Why are you so different? Why do you talk differently? Why do you eat different food? Where are you going to live? When are you going home? You shouldn't get involved in our world. You don't have a place in it. You shouldn't get married and have sex with our daughters, et cetera.

I mean a profound rejection by the so-called mother country of its own so-called children. That is how I encountered it. Well, what am I supposed to do? Should I go back to Jamaica and live there? I find it difficult to make a place for myself, to realize my own identity there. Or should I stay where I've gone to as a student and begin to understand, to be involved in political events, and try to change my life and the world around me from that position? And for various personal reasons, I chose the latter. I chose to do that rather than to go back home.

One of the reasons why I did that was in the first few months that I was in London I suddenly saw coming out of the tube station, the railway station, a mass of ordinary Jamaican people. I thought to myself, "What are they doing here? This is London. What are they doing over here?" So this is the beginning of post-black migration to Britain. So after a while, I thought, "Well, you don't need to go home to fight this problem. It's just come to greet you from the past in the world you are now living in."

So I spent much of the rest of my life identifying with this cause trying to understand how they are socially oppressed or economically oppressed, examining how they are being exploited, and looking at the struggles that they've waged in order to change their situation. I've identified myself as a black subject—I feel now that goes back to your very first point: a diasporic subject is someone who has to live his or her life in two worlds.

I never forget the past. I feel Jamaica as I did eighty years ago when I was born; I love it. My childhood memories of it are very deep. My memories of the landscape and of the people are extremely rich and positive, but I couldn't live there anymore. Now, the place I've gone to has all the disadvantages you can imagine.

They are immigrants and they're people like me. I came to recognize myself as an immigrant. I moved to settle somewhere else. They (Jamaican immigrants) came largely for economic reasons, and I went largely because I got a scholarship to study abroad. It doesn't matter. We were both in a new culture. There's no way to forget the past. And there's no way in which I wouldn't say we are all changed by having to make a life in a new world under different historical circumstance and among people very different from the people we grew up with.

Orelus: Between the time when you left Jamaica and now, have you seen any change in the way people of color, particularly black people, in the UK are treated?

Hall: Yes and no. Remember we talked a little bit earlier about institutional racism? And you asked whether I thought there had been some advances in that area? I said modest advances, but the problem hasn't gone away. And that's the answer I would give you. Yes, it happens. When I first arrived, one would never have found a black presenter on the British broadcast here. There were no black presenters.

One would never have found a black footballer. One would never have found a black celebrity. I had never seen a black comic among television. I had never seen a black actor working, acting Shakespeare at the national theater. So there has been a penetration of black people into the British society slowly, slowly, and slowly. It's come to be taken for granted that black people are here.

When I came, it wasn't taken for granted. It was taken for granted that we would go back home as soon as possible. Nobody thinks we're going to go back home. We're here, and we're here for good. Lots of people don't like it, but they are going to have to tolerate it. So that's a bit of a change. That's the effects of colonization and racism with respect to black people. Has that profoundly changed? My answer is no.

There have been improvements. And I don't think it's worth pretending that there haven't been. There have been significant changes: there are black presenters, black actors, and lots of black footballers. There are more black people in sports than business rooms, but never mind that. That's one of the places where the things begin to show up. So there have been advances, but the idea that the advances have made such a difference that we are in a totally different situation, I don't believe it.

Orelus: Are you hopeful that someday, like in the U.S., you will have a black president in the UK? Do you think that might happen just like it happened in the U.S.?

Hall: Yes, it could happen. There are black and Asian members of the parliament now. There are people who are ministers of the crown. So why shouldn't one of them be so outstanding to lead the party, his or her party? And why shouldn't she or he be lucky enough, work hard enough, or be distinguished enough to be asked to be prime minister? Why not? If you asked Abraham Lincoln, will there be a black president, what do you think he would have said? So if you asked Mr. Cameron, my current prime minister: Do you think there'll be a black prime minister next time around? He would say: of course not. These days if I said: Can you see a time coming when we could have a black prime minister? I bet he would have to say yes, but he wouldn't like it very much. Yes, I can see it.

Orelus: While you were explaining the reason why you ended up going to the UK, you made a statement that caught my attention. You said you couldn't live in Jamaica. Can you tell me a little bit more why you felt at the time you couldn't live there?

Hall: No, it's too complicated of a story to go into any detail. I gave you a hint when I said I was brought up in a family, in a family culture, which did not identify itself as black, share a unity with a vast majority of ordinary Jamaican black people. I revolted against that culture, which is still hard to identify. It's still difficult to feel well I wasn't just an ordinary black person.

I was a black person, Jamaican, brought up in an alienated colonial atmosphere. That creates tensions and shapes one's identity. I just didn't want to face that for the rest of my life. I couldn't easily resolve that dilemma. I said to myself: change the scenery to see if you can find a life where you can express really who you really are, and who you want to be more accurately rather than living in that familial domestic setting in Jamaica where you were brought up. Go and do it.

I know it's not popular nor thought of as the right thing to say. But I couldn't live in Jamaica, and that's the truth. To tell the truth a lot of people know in their hearts that's true. I have very good friends who have lived and worked in England for fifty or sixty years who went back home to spend their retirement in Jamaica. And you know what? They come back to England every few months—they belong to both worlds.

They can't really go back to Jamaica. They've seen London. They've been to New York. So you can't refashion yourself. You have to find an honest, a just, and a tolerable way of living with who you are and try to be who you are and make the best of it. If I'm able to do that better in this society than that society, so be it. And my loyalty to Jamaica won't make me say anything different.

Orelus: I sort of feel the same way about living in the U.S. I don't know if I mentioned that earlier: I was born and grew up in Haiti. I moved to the U.S.

in my early twenties. Obviously, I wanted to stay in Haiti, but the political situation and the social-economic problems that the whole country was facing compelled me to leave the country to seek better opportunities overseas.

Hall: So, you have an answer to the question you asked me about your own life. I responded to you partly because to be honest that's what I suspected.

Orelus: It's a dilemma for me.

Hall: It's a dilemma for me too.

Orelus: It's a dilemma because I feel I should have stayed in Haiti. On the other hand, I knew staying there would not have been the best option given what was and is still going on there.

Hall: In some ways it's a tragedy.

Orelus: Yes, that's correct, because I don't see myself going back to Haiti now.

Hall: For me, that's how it is. I came here when I was nineteen. I'm eighty, and I will be eighty-one next year. I just couldn't go back to Jamaica. I wouldn't know how to start living in Jamaica at this stage. Sometimes I think you can't really go home again. In a metaphorical sense, once you leave home you can't climb back into that loving familiar intimate world any longer. You're out in the world. You go to battle with it.

Orelus: That's correct. I hope to be able to go back when I retire but I still have my doubts.

Hall: Do what my friends do. You go back. You love being in Haiti again, but you come to the U.S. every now and again, the other life that you had. Haiti is a very interesting place. I speak not as a Haitian, but as a Caribbean. It's a fascinating society: the history, the culture, the people, and cultural practices. I mean I've never seen such extensive synchronism between African religion and Catholic religion as I saw in Haiti. People are moving between African ritual and the Catholic mass in front of my eyes. The two worlds right there. When I went to a market in Port-au-Prince, I thought this is just like Africa. So Haiti knows both of those things.

But in other parts of the more recent French empires, like Martinique, I think I'm in a bloody black Paris. People are passing me in the street, it is cold, and they've got a baguette under their arms, for god's sake.

They're dressed in a very swish Parisian way. So you know culture is extraordinary, always changing. It combines different forms; it brings unexpected things together. That's just what it is.

Orelus: Speaking of culture, in your opinion, when and in what way might some cultural practices "become a problem"?

Hall: Well, it depends on what cultural practices you have in mind.

Orelus: Let me give you an example. In some countries in Africa, they practice female genital mutilation.

Hall: I thought that was what you were going to ask me. This is a very difficult dilemma. I'm against genital female mutilation. I think there's a long, too long history of men interfering in the independence of women's lives. I mean, I don't see any women trying to alter sexual activities or equipment of men. So why should society now still want to push women into that situation? So on that specific practice, I just don't have any time for it. Why and what's the principle behind what you're asking? On the one hand, there is the urge toward greater acceptance of cultural practices that are not the same as yours. We live in a more culturally relativistic position than the past.

Orelus: And that's a good thing?

Hall: I'm not sure. And one of the reasons why I'm not sure is because I think the world has come off globalization and colonialism and so on. You can't isolate yourself, and we treat women like that because we're not moving between the two worlds. Cultural relativism is a good instinct, but you can't take it too far. Universalism, which is the opposite, has its challenges.

Is there one standard of universal values and practices to which everybody should obey? That's dictatorial. That's authoritarian. I don't believe there is one set of practices, one system of values. The real problem about that position is that universalism, when you look at it very closely, always turns out to be Western values, Western practices. So the power moves one way. I'm not a universalist, so I don't want to see everybody behaving exactly the same way. Let's just take another example, which is not as violent and extreme as genital mutilation. Let's take the wearing of the hijab.

What do I think about it? It's not what Western women wear. Now we live in a more multicultural society, a more multicultural world. Why shouldn't some of them wear what they like to wear here in the West? They're not offending me. I don't think it is any longer a sign of female dependency and subordination to men; but I don't think it's that any longer in the West; it may have been in the past.

I see young women wearing the hijab; they are very independent, highly educated, and very ambitious; they're not being held back any longer. Perhaps in the countries where they come from that is still a sign of female inequality and an injustice towards women. I'm not sure if it will go on being so. It's very hard to strike this balance between a universal set of values, which seraphically turn out to be Western values smuggled into universal values, and a cultural relativism. The practices you referred to, I think they are inhumane and socially unjust.

Orelus: Let me ask you one last question, actually two. What would you like to be remembered for?

Hall: I would like to be remembered for what I said—I am an intellectual; that's my role in life. I don't think it deserves special privileges. It's just what I do, what I do best. I would like to think that I've fulfilled my intellectual duty to the fullest possibility. That is to say that I learned and found opportunities to speak truth to power. Secondly, I would like to think however indirectly I've contributed to creating a more racially, sexually, and socially just world in some way—a tiny contribution. An individual can't contribute very much, but I would like people to think I was on that side of history.

Orelus: What advice would you give young scholars, like myself, who are trying and eager to make some kind of change not only in the academic world but also in the world beyond the ivory tower?

Hall: What I can tell you is to dedicate yourself to that purpose every morning. I don't know what to say. I mean, you know what your duty is as a public intellectual, a citizen, and a member of an oppressed group. You know what your duty is, do it.

Conclusion

There is a wide body of scholars that examine social justice issues. These scholars explore varied forms of social injustices that have affected the lives of people, particularly those from poor socioeconomic and stigmatized linguistic and racial backgrounds.

In *Readings for Diversity and Social Justice,* for example, Adams et al. (2012) examine the intersection of racism, sexism, classism, ageism, and ableism, among other isms, and show ways and the degree to which these intersected forms of oppression affect the lives of people, particularly historically marginalized groups. Similarly, in *Teaching for Social Justice*, North (2009) explores the manner in which social justice–oriented teachers might help students develop critical awareness and consciousness about various forms of oppression.

Finally, in *Rethinking Race, Class, Language, and Gender*, Orelus (2011) offers a critical analysis of intersected forms of race-, social class-, language-, and gender-based oppression in schools and society as a whole. This book analyzes similar social issues and concerns but provides a more global and diverse perspective on these issues.

Specifically, the content of this book provides both a non-Western and Western perspective on pertinent social justice issues, including the marginalization of youth in society; the misrepresentation of minority groups in the media; the resources gap between privileged and poor students; women's oppression; and the struggle of immigrants and colonized subjects to maintain their native tongue and cultural heritage. Members of these oppressed groups have often been subject to, and have been resisting, racial, socioeconomic, and linguistic apartheid in schools and society.

In the introduction, many factors linked to social justice are examined and various questions about this notion are asked, such as: (1) Social justice for whom? (2) Whose interests does it serve? (3) Can this term be a reality for those who have been historically pushed to the margins in society? In posing these questions, the goal was to deconstruct the concept *social justice*. Social justice is a very complex term, and it is inextricably connected to many important issues, such as sexual and religious freedom; socioeconomic, gender, and racial equality; and workers' rights.

All of which fall under the umbrella term: human rights. For example, denying people the right to have access to quality education and health care, decent employment, and to practice their religion is a violation of their human rights. Stated otherwise, violating one's human rights is nothing but social injustice. Grant and Gibson state (2010), "Human rights cannot be divorced from social and economic arrangements—justice and rights are inextricably linked" (cited in Chapman & Hobbel, p. 25).

This book aims at creating a holistic space for readers to start engaging in genuine dialogues about both the promises and the perils of social justice. For the privileged, especially the few who have monopolized the wealth of the world, social justice might mean something. But for historically oppressed groups, it might not mean much, if anything. As long as webs of oppression continue to occur affecting their livelihood, discussions revolved around social justice issues must continue to take place in school, churches, at home, and beyond.

The social justice educators and public intellectuals involved in this book do not merely point out socioeconomic, racial, linguistic, gender, and educational injustices that have been committed against marginalized groups in society but they also offer alternatives to these injustices. By saying so, it is not meant that this book is a panacea containing *the* solution to all social inequities. Far from this pretense. Rather, it is an invitation to further engage these issues, providing alternative proposals.

This book offers various stances on social justice issues taken by public activist intellectuals and committed educators. These intellectuals and educators point out the manner in which multiple forms of social oppression intersect, in both hidden and visible ways, to affect the lives of oppressed groups living in disfranchised communities. This book seeks to shed light on various manifestations of social injustice while at the same time inspiring critical, radical thoughts for sociopolitical action leading to social change. All in all, this book hopes to accomplish the following goals:

1. To denounce social injustices occurring in schools and society at large.
2. To contribute to political consciousness and awareness among readers from diverse backgrounds about racial, socioeconomic, educational, and political challenges facing oppressed groups.
3. To help readers understand ways and the degree to which various forms of oppression, such as racism, sexism, classism, xenophobia, colonialism, and Western imperialism, intersect to systematically affect the lives of historically marginalized communities.
4. Finally, to inspire critical thoughts leading to political action and social movements aimed at eradicating social injustices.

REFERENCES

Adams, M. (2010). "Roots of Social Justice Pedagogies in Social Movements." In T. Chapman & N. Hobbel (Eds.), *Social Justice Pedagogy across the Curriculum: The Practice of Freedom* (pp. 36–85). New York: Routledge.

Alexander, M. (2010). *The New Jim Crow: Mass Incarceration in the Age of Colorblindness.* New York: New Press.

Fanon, F. (1963). *The Wretched of the Earth.* New York: Grove Press.

Gee, J. (2010). *How to Do Discourse Analysis: A Toolkit.* New York: Routledge.

Grant, K., & Gibson, M. (2010). "'These Are Revolutionary Times': Human Rights, Social Justice, and Popular Protest." In T. Chapman & N. Hobbel (Eds.), *Social Justice Pedagogy across the Curriculum: The Practice of Freedom* (pp. 1–35). New York: Routledge.

Orelus, P. W. (Ed.) (2011). *Rethinking Race, Class, Language, and Gender: A Dialogue with Noam Chomsky and Other Leading Scholars.* Lanham, MD: Rowman & Littlefield.

About the Author

Pierre Wilbert Orelus is associate professor in the Curriculum and Instruction Department at New Mexico State University. He is the former program chair and current co-chair of both the Paulo Freire and Postcolonial SIGs (special interest groups) at American Educational Research Association. Orelus has received several awards for his scholarship, including New Mexico State University Exceptional Achievements in Creative Scholarly Activity Award (2013).

His scholarly research is interdisciplinary, examining ways and the degree to which ways race, language, and power intersect to influence student learning and people's life chances and opportunities in general, particularly for those of working class background. Since completing his doctorate in 2008, Orelus has written ten scholarly books, edited and co-edited eight books, and published twenty-five referred articles and book chapters combined. His articles have been published in respected journals, such as *Journal of Black Studies*; *Race, Gender, and Class*; and *Diaspora, Indigenous, and Minority Education*. His most recent books include *Race, Power, and the Obama Legacy* (2015) and *Language, Race, and Power in Schools: A Critical Discourse Analysis* (2016). In endorsing Orelus' book, *The Agony of Masculinity*, the prominent African American scholar, Cornel West, states, "Orelus is an intellectual freedom fighter whose deep insights and sharp analyses of institutional racism and black masculinity deserve our attention." Orelus is one the few talented young scholars who wrote his first acclaimed book while he was still a graduate student. The national and international recognition of Orelus' scholarly work is shown through several talk invitations he has received to deliver plenary and keynote speeches at major national conferences, like CABE (California Association of Bilingual Education), and international conferences in Greece, Canada, Spain, and Italy. His peers and prominent scholars have rated Orelus as a gifted scholar and prolific writer.

About the Interviewees

Rodolfo Acuña, professor emeritus, received his Ph.D. in 1968 from the University of Southern California in Latin American Studies. A janitor and then a teacher in the Los Angeles City Schools from 1956–1965, he transferred to the community colleges where he taught for three years. In 1969, Acuña was the founding chair of Chicano Studies at San Fernando Valley State (today California State University Northridge), which is the largest in the United States with thirty tenured professors. *Black Issues In Higher Education* selected Acuña one of the "100 Most Influential Educators of the 20th Century;" three of his works have received the Gustavus Myers Award for an Outstanding Book on Race Relations in North America. *Black Issues in Higher Education* named him one of the most influential scholars of the previous century; in 2014 The National Education Association honored him for outstanding work in America's human and civil rights; in March 2016, Diversity in Higher Education presented him with the John Hope Franklin Award; he has also received the Distinguished Scholar Award from National Association for Chicano Studies, and numerous academic and community service awards, such as an *homenaje* from the University of Guadalajara Feria Internacional del Libro and the State of Guadalajara, Mexico, for the Outstanding Scholar of U.S.–Mexico Studies; the Emil Freed Award for Community Service from the Southern California Social Science Library; the Founder's Award for Community Service from the Liberty Hill Foundation; academic fellowships from the American Council of Learned Societies Award; the Rockefeller Humanities Scholar's Grant. Acuña was also a founder of the Latin American Civic Association Headstart program and a cofounder of the Labor Community Strategy Center. Acuña was under contract as a columnist for the *Los Angeles Herald–Express, La Opinión,* and the *Los Angeles Times* from 1986–1992, and has contributed to leading newspapers and magazines. He was featured in *Counterpunch,* a magazine founded by the late Alexander Cockburn. Among his best-known books are *Occupied America: A History of Chicanos* (Eighth Edition, 2015); *The Making Of Chicana/o Studies: In the Trenches of Academe* (2011); *Latino Voices* (2008); *Corridors of Migration: the Odyssey of Mexican Laborers, 1600–1933* (2007); *US Latinos: An Inquiry* (2003); and *Guide to Occupied America*. Acuña has written three children's books and has three other books in production.

Molefi Kete Asante is a Diopian intellectual who is currently professor and chair, Department of Africology at Temple University. He is also president of Molefi Kete Asante Institute for Afrocentric Studies and international organizer for Afrocentricity International. Asante is a guest professor, Zhejiang University, Hangzhou, China and Professor Extraordinarius at the University of South Africa. Inspired by his meeting with Cheikh Anta Diop in 1981, Asante has published 83 books; among the most recent are *The History of Africa, African Pyramids of Knowledge, Facing South to Africa,* and *As I Run Toward Africa*. Asante has published more than 500 articles and is considered the most published African American scholar as well as one of the most distinguished authors in the African world.

Asante was born in Valdosta, Georgia, of Sudanese (Nubian) and Nigerian (Yoruba) heritage. He completed his M.A. at Pepperdine and received his Ph.D. from the University of California, Los Angeles (UCLA) at the age of 26, and was appointed a full professor at the age of 30 at the State University of New York at Buffalo. Asante was the president of the Civil Rights Organization, the Student Non-Violent Coordinating Committee chapter at UCLA in the 1960s and is the founding editor of the *Journal of Black Studies* (1969). At Temple University, he created the first Ph.D. program in Africology and Africana Studies in 1988. He has directed more than 120 Ph.D. dissertations in the fields of Communication and African American Studies. His works on African language, multiculturalism, and human culture and philosophy have been cited and reviewed by journals such as the *Africalogical Perspectives, Quarterly Journal of Speech, Journal of Black Studies, Journal of Communication, American Scholar,* and *International Journal of Pan African Thought*. The *Utne Reader* called him one of the "100 Leading Thinkers" in America. He is the founder of the theory of Afrocentricity and the creator of the first doctoral program in African American Studies. Asante has appeared on numerous television programs in Africa, America, and Europe. He has received many awards and honors for scholarship and political activism, including the International Cheikh Anta Diop Award for outstanding scholarship given by the Diopian Institute. He regularly consults with heads of state in Africa and has become one of the most sought after lecturers on the United States of Africa. In 1995 he was made a traditional king, Nana Okru Asante Peasah, Kyidomhene of Tafo, Akyem, Ghana. He was recently made a Wanadu of the Court of Hassimi Maiga, the Amiru of Gao Songhay. He is the International Organizer for Afrocentricity International, a global African organization involved in establishing new pathways to African identity and culture. Asante is one of the major professional trainers of Afrocentric teachers for urban schools. He is a poet, novelist, dramatist, and a painter.

Noam Chomsky is an American linguist, philosopher, cognitive scientist, logician, political commentator, social justice activist, and anarcho-syndicalist advocate. Sometimes described as the "father of modern linguistics," Chomsky is also a major figure in analytic philosophy. He has spent most of his career at the Massachusetts Institute of Technology (MIT), where he is currently professor emeritus, and has authored over one hundred books. He has been described as a prominent cultural figure, and was voted the "world's top public intellectual" in a 2005 poll.

Antonia Darder is a distinguished international Freirian scholar. She holds the Leavey Presidential Endowed Chair of Ethics and Moral Leadership at Loyola Marymount University, Los Angeles, and is professor emerita of education policy, organization, and leadership at the University of Illinois, Urbana-Champaign. Her scholarship focuses on issues of racism, political economy, social justice, and education. Her work critically engages the contributions of Paulo Freire to our understanding of inequalities in schools and society. Darder's critical theory of biculturalism links questions of culture, power, and pedagogy to social justice concerns in education. In her scholarship on ethics and moral issues, she articulates a critical theory of leadership for social justice and community empowerment. She is the author of numerous books and articles in the field, including *Culture and Power in the Classroom* (Twentieth Anniversary Edition); *Reinventing Paulo Freire: A Pedagogy of Love*; *A Dissident Voice: Essays on Culture, Pedagogy, and Power*; and *Freire and Education*. She is also coauthor of *After Race: Racism After Multiculturalism* and coeditor of *The Critical Pedagogy Reader, Latinos and Education: A Critical Reader* and the *International Critical Pedagogy Reader*.

George Sefa Dei is professor of social justice education at the Ontario Institute for Studies in Education of the University of Toronto (OISE/UT). He is the director for the Centre for Integrative Anti-Racism Studies at the University of Toronto, Canada. Dei was awarded a 2015 Carnegie African Diaspora fellowship. The Carnegie African Diaspora Fellowship Program is a prestigious scholar fellowship program for educational projects at African higher-education institutions. Dei's teaching and research interests are in the areas of antiracism, minority schooling, international development, anticolonial thought, and Indigenous knowledge systems.

Dei is the recipient of many awards. He received the 2014 Distinguished Teaching Award at OISE/UT for excellence in teaching over the years. He is also the 2014 recipient of the Ludwik and Estelle Jus Memorial Human Rights Prize from the University of Toronto for his internationally recognized work on antiracism and social justice. His other awards include the Race, Gender, and Class Project Academic Award 2002 in New Orleans. He also received the African-Canadian Outstanding Achievement in Education from *Pride* magazine in Toronto in 2003, and the City of Toronto's William P. Hubbard Award for Race Relations in 2003. He is also the 2006 recipient of the Planet Africa Renaissance Award for his professional achievements in the field of African education, antiracism, and youth and the 2007 Canadian Alliance of Black Educators Award for Excellence in Education and Community Development. Finally, in June of 2007, Dei was installed as a traditional chief in Ghana. He is the Gyaasehene of the town of Asokore, in the New Juaben Traditional Area of Ghana.

James Paul Gee is the Mary Lou Fulton Presidential Professor of Literacy Studies and Regents' Professor at Arizona State University. He is a member of the National Academy of Education. His book *Sociolinguistics and Literacies* (Fourth Edition, 2011) was one of the founding documents in the formation of the New Literacy Studies. His book *An Introduction to Discourse Analysis* (Third Edition, 2011) brings together his work on a methodology for studying communication in its cultural settings, an approach that has been widely influential over the last two decades. His most recent books have dealt with video games, language, and learning. *What Video Games Have to Teach Us about Learning and Literacy* (Second Edition, 2007) argues that good video games are designed to enhance learning through effective learning principles supported by research in the learning sciences. *Situated Language and Learning* (2004) places video games within an overall theory of learning and literacy and shows how they can help us in thinking about the reform of schools. *The Anti-Education Era: Creating Smarter Students through Digital Media* appeared in 2013 and *Literacy and Education* in 2014. Gee has published widely in journals in linguistics, psychology, the social sciences, and education.

Henry A. Giroux currently holds a chair for Scholarship in the Public Interest at McMaster University in the English and Cultural Studies Department. He is also the Paulo Freire Distinguished Scholar Chair in Critical Pedagogy and holds a Distinguished Visiting Professorship at Ryerson University. In 2012, he was named by the *Toronto Star* as one of the top twelve Canadians Changing the Way We Think. His most recent books include *The Violence of Organized Forgetting: Thinking Beyond America's Disimagination Machine* (2014); *Neoliberalism's War Against Higher Education* (2014); *Dangerous Thinking in the Age of the New Authoritarianism* (2015); and *Disposable Futures: The Seduction of Violence in the Age of the Spectacle* (coauthored with Brad Evans, 2015).

Maxine Greene, an American educational philosopher, author, social activist, and teacher, valued experiential learning in its "entirety" and influenced thousands of educators to bring the vitality of the arts to teachers and children. For Greene, art provided a conduit to meaning-making, a way of making sense of the world.

Greene graduated from the Berkeley Institute in 1934, earned a B.A. from Barnard College, Columbia University, in 1938, and earned her M.A. (1949) and Ph.D. (1955) from New York University. She taught at New York University, Montclair State College, and Brooklyn College. In 1965, she joined the faculty at Teachers College, Columbia University. In 1973 she was one of the signers of the Humanist Manifesto II. As Philosopher-in-Residence of Lincoln Center Institute for the Arts in Education from 1976 to 2012, Greene conducted workshops (especially in literature as art) and lectures at LCI's summer sessions. In 2003, she founded the Maxine Greene Foundation for Social Imagination, the Arts, and Education. The foundation supports the creation and appreciation of works that embody fresh social visions. Its goal is "to generate inquiry, imagination and the creation of art works by diverse people." Grants of up to $10,000 are awarded to educators and artists. In 2005, she inspired the creation for the High School of Arts, Imagination and Inquiry in association with LCI and New Visions for Public Schools. The school encourages students to expand their imaginative capacities in the arts and other subject areas. Greene was past president of the American Educational Research Association, Philosophy of Education Society, American Educational Studies Association, and the Middle Atlantic States Philosophy of Education Society.

Stuart Hall was a Jamaican-born cultural theorist, political activist, and sociologist who lived and worked in the United Kingdom from 1951. Hall, along with Richard Hoggart and Raymond Williams, was one of the founding figures of the school of thought that is now known as British Cultural Studies or the Birmingham School of Cultural Studies.

In the 1950s, Hall was a founder of the influential *New Left Review*. At the invitation of Hoggart, Hall joined the Centre for Contemporary Cultural Studies at Birmingham University in 1964. Hall took over from Hoggart as acting director of the Centre in 1968, became its director in 1972, and remained there until 1979. While at the Centre, Hall is credited with playing a role in expanding the scope of cultural studies to deal with race and gender, and with helping to incorporate new ideas derived from the work of French theorists like Michel Foucault.

Hall left the Centre in 1979 to become a professor of sociology at the Open University. He was president of the British Sociological Association 1995–1997. Hall retired from the Open University in 1997 and was professor emeritus. The British newspaper *The Observer* called him "one of the country's leading cultural theorists."

Kevin Kumashiro, Ph.D., is dean of the School of Education at the University of San Francisco. He is a leading expert on educational policy, school reform, teacher preparation, and educational equity and social justice, with a wide-ranging list of accomplishments nationally and internationally as an educator, leader, and media expert. He has taught in schools and colleges across the United States and abroad and has served as a consultant for school districts, organizations, and state and federal agencies. He is an award-winning author and editor of ten books, including *Troubling Education* (recipient of the 2003 Gustavus Myers Outstanding Book Award), *Against Common Sense: Teaching and Learning toward Social Justice,* and *Bad Teacher! How Blaming Teachers Distorts the Bigger Picture.* His recent awards include the 2013 Mid-Career Scholar Award from the American Educational Research Association (AERA) Division K on Teaching and Teacher Education, the 2014 Engaged Scholar Award from the Association for Asian American Studies, and the 2015 Distinguished Scholar Award from the AERA Scholars of Color.

Gayatri Chakravorty Spivak is a university professor at Columbia University, where she is a founding member of the school's Institute for Comparative Literature and Society. She is best known for the essay "Can the Subaltern Speak?" considered a founding text of postcolonialism, and for her translation of and introduction to Jacques Derrida's *De la Grammatologie.* In 2012, Spivak was awarded the Kyoto Prize in Arts and Philosophy for being "a critical theorist and educator speaking for the humanities against intellectual colonialism in relation to the globalized world." In 2013, she received the Padma Bhushan, the third-highest civilian award given by the Republic of India.

www.ingramcontent.com/pod-product-compliance
Lightning Source LLC
Chambersburg PA
CBHW020002290326
41935CB00007B/278